AF731801

"*Europe After Enlargement: Economic Challenges for EU and India* by Jean-Joseph Boillot collects varies ideas and comes at a time of changes not only for Europe, when the continent is *de facto* and *de jure* overcoming its past divisions and extending into the largest single market in the world. But for the world at large, at a time when the re-organisation of the European productive space interacts with globalisation and the emerging and consolidation of new powers. Hence, this publication comes at a time of change for the EU/India partnership as well, at a time when their relations enter a new phase of development and become strategic. Jean-Joseph Boillot collects analysis of the new geographical trends in the European economy and focuses the debate surrounding the extension of the European Union by highlighting the discovery of new internal sources by the European competitiveness by means of EU enlargement and by stressing challenges ahead. In doing so, Mr Boillot's publication stimulates the debate and looks at the possible European development and at the challenges ahead also from an Indian perspective, raising interesting points for discussions and further investigation into the economic dynamics of this historic EU enlargement."

— **Francisco da Câmara Gomes**

Ambassador, European Union, Delegation of the European Commission to India, Bhutan, Maldives, Nepal and Sri Lanka

"As India opens up to the world, Indians will need better information on those parts of the world that matter. Jean-Joseph Boillot's book fills an urgent need. Its discussion of the new members of the European Union is particularly valuable: they are potentially India's competitors of the EU market, but could be transformed by more perceptive businessmen into bases for penetrating the bastion of the EU."

— **Ashok V. Desai**

Consultant Editor, The Telegraph, New Delhi

"This book provides a lucid explanation to the process of European integration and its impact on the Indian trade and capital flows with respect to Europe. The author has shown a depth of understanding of economic problems in both the eastern and the western European region. I recommend it highly for the scholars interested in European integration and policymakers and diplomats of both Europe and India."

— **Prof. B.B. Bhattacharya**

Vice-Chancellor, Jawaharlal Nehru University, New Delhi

"Enlargement — in fact, the reunification of Europe — has changed the nature of the EU. Understanding what it means and where it leads to is essential for all the partners of Europe. Having for a decade observed the enlargement process from the West and from the East, Jean-Joseph Boillot was uniquely equipped to analyse it and grasp its consequences. His comprehensive and timely book is an achievement."

— **Prof. Jean Pisani-Ferry**

Director, Brussels European and Global Economic Laboratory (Bruegel)
Professor, University of Paris-Dauphine

Contd....

...Comments continued...

"A fascinating and eminently readable account of Europe's eastward expansion and its emergence as a world economic power in the closing years of the twentieth century. The opportunities that this transformation opens up are tremendous and this book is a welcome wake-up call for entrepreneurs, policymakers and analysts. Backed by a wealth of data, it presents new perspectives on the robust economies of the new Europe."

— **Prof. Balveer Arora**
Former Rector & Pro Vice-Chancellor Coordinator, UGC-SAP,
Centre for Political Studies, Jawaharlal Nehru University, New Delhi

"This volume by Jean-Joseph Boillot on 'Europe After Enlargement: Economic Challenges for EU and India' provides analytical insights on the process of enlargement from the perspective of someone who has been intimately connected with the process from his vantage perch in Budapest when the terms of enlargement were actually negotiated. At the same time, Jean-Joseph, also has a unique knowledge of how the Indian system works, having started his India affair nearly twenty years ago. He is, therefore, able to present intricacies of the European enlargement process and its implications for India in a manner that is immediately comprehensible to the Indian reader. A book well worth reading by all those who believe that a multi-polar world is a more benign environment for India's future."

— **Rajiv Kumar**
Chief Economist Confederation of Indian Industry (CII), New Delhi

"As a person living and working in India, the book held great interest for me, as I think it certainly will for Indian managers looking to do business with Europe. I found the details of the discussions in the developing links between the Central and Eastern European Countries (CEEC) extremely educative, throwing light on the complex web of the nature of the transaction, the character of the protagonists, the products, technology, location and ownership issues. Given its very contemporary context, the book brings out very well the evolving nature of these relationships and what the implications can be for players located outside of Europe, as for instance in India. Historically, Indian business who had engaged with the former Eastern Europe had done so in the context of the Warsaw Pact bloc, where business success depended on one particular method of managing the environment, namely the state and its apparatus. Finding a niche in today's highly dynamic and rapidly evolving CEEC, Indian businesses have an opportunity of expanding their potential engagement with Europe as a whole, benefiting from the privileged status of the accession countries in the EU. But in the event that they do not, there appears to be a possibility that Indian business might find it difficult to maintain their existing market share in the trade activity of Europe. This is a must-read book for all businesspersons, academics and analysts from the subcontinent with an interest in Europe. A perusal of the book provides a rich haul of ideas that might be pursued further with considerable profit — by both, the businessperson and the researcher."

— **Samitra Chaudhuri**
Economic Advisor with ICRA and member of the Economic
Advisory Council to the Prime Minister of India

Europe after enlargement

* *

Economic challenges for EU and India

Jean-Joseph Boillot

Academic Foundation
NEW DELHI

JEAN-JOSEPH BOILLOT is Professor of Social Sciences, and holds a Ph.D. in Development Economics. His dissertation was on India's economic development since Independence. From 1990, he has been Economic Advisor with the French Ministry of Finance on the main challenging regions of the world: Eastern Europe, Russia and CIS, East Asia and again Eastern Europe for the last EU enlargement negotiations. In 2003, he joined the French Treasury as Financial Advisor for India and South Asia, based in New Delhi. He is author of more than 20 books and of many articles on various fields of economics, particularly International and Development Economics, and on India and China. He is member of the Editorial Committee of the Monthly Alternatives Economiques, the EuroIndia Center and Confrontation Europe. He is married and has two daughters.

This edition is published in India in 2006 by
ACADEMIC FOUNDATION
4772-73 / 23 Bharat Ram Road, (23 Ansari Road),
Darya Ganj, New Delhi - 110 002 (India).
Phones : 23245001 / 02 / 03 / 04.
Fax : +91-11-23245005.
E-mail : academic@vsnl.com
www.academicfoundation.com

The first four chapters of this book have been translated from French of the corresponding chapters of : L'Union Européenne élargie, un défi économique pour tous, published by La Documentation Française, Paris © 2003 (copyright for the French edition).

Copyright © 2006
Academic Foundation, New Delhi.

All rights reserved.
No part of this book shall be reproduced, stored in a retrieval system, or transmitted by any means, electronic, mechanical, photocopying, recording, or otherwise, without the prior written permission of the publisher

Europe After Enlargement: Economic Challenges for EU and India
by Jean-Joseph Boillot

ISBN 81-7188-509-8

Printed and bound in India

Contents

Introduction 11

1. The Institutional and Economic Rationale Behind Enlargement 15

Institutional Rationality: The EU Methodology
From Copenhagen (June 1993) to Copenhagen (December 2002)
The Four Pillars of the Enlargement Process
The Association Agreements (or the European Agreements)
The Negotiations Framework: The 31 Chapters of the 'Acquis Communautaire'
The Process of Financial Support: The EU Programmes
A Process of Institutional Support: The Reinforcement of the Administrative Capacities
Economic Rationality: A Twin Gain for Europe
Ensuring that the Central and East European Countries Catch-up: Convergence
The 2000-2002 Growth Cycle Substantiates the Process of Convergence and its Challenges
The Masses and very Diverse Standards of Living
Benefits to the EU15 Group should not be Under-Estimated
Distribution of the Costs-Benefits of Enlargement: A Sensitive Subject

2. The Virtuous Logic of Integration: FDI and Consumption Catching-up 51

A Region that is Becoming Important for FDI Flows Towards Emerging Countries
The Increasing Global Attractiveness of the CEECs
Human Capital and its Cost: A Picture of Contrasts
The Importance of the Institutional Environment
The Proximity of EU15: A Powerful Factor of Attraction
Competitiveness of the CEEC and Competitiveness of Greater Europe
A FDI Potential which has not even Remotely been Achieved in the Early 2000s
The Initial Effects of FDI on Industrial Restructuring
FDI, Bridging the Productivity Gap and Setting the Successful Tempo of Convergence

...CONTD. ..

The Consumption-Distribution Synergy
The Rise in Consumption Levels since the Mid-Nineties
Disparities between and within the CEEC Countries
Standardisation and Specificity of Consumption Modes

3. Trade as a Means of European Integration 85

Normalisation of Trade and Geographical Reorientation
The Re-direction of Trade Flows Towards the European Union will Continue
The Revival of Intra-CEEC Trade: A Crucial Component of the Intra-EU27 Trade
CEEC-Russia Trade: Are Legacy and Geographical Proximity an Asset?
Enlargement and the New Economic Geography of Continental Europe
The New Economic Geography of Europe: Five Belts and the Two New Expanding Axes
The Nordic Basin or the Mare Balticum
The Central European Belt or Mitteleuropa
The South-East European Basin
The Old Post-war European Community Centre
The Iberian Space
The French Case
The Reinforcement of Sectoral Specialisation
But the Dynamics of Country-wise
Specialisation is Unequal

4. Sectoral Dynamics 117

Textile-Garments: Inroads into a Global Industry, but for How Long?
The Regionalisation of Global Trade in Favour of the CEECs
Shorter Cycle: Mediterranean-CEEC Versus Asia
Clothing: The Take-off of Short Supply Cycles in Europe
Can Wages Convergence Put a Brake on Textile Development in the CEECs
The Emergence of a Complete Textile Chain will Probably Run Up Against the Shortcomings of Local Industrialists
Furniture: Old Suppliers and a Local Demand that is Gradually Gaining in Strength
An Export-Driven Recovery Rendered Fragile by the Cyclical Downturn in the European Business Climate
Domestic Markets – New Opportunities for Local Firms but also for West European Firms
NICT (or IT, Information Technologies): The Difficult Conversion of Supply and the Unequal Convergence of Demand

A Promising Beginning Interrupted by the Internet Bubble Crisis of the Second Millennium
A Slow and Unequal Catching-up of the Demand for NTIC
The Catching-up of Computer Related Equipment has Slowed Down
The Adaptation Crisis in the East European Iron and Steel Industry
The Emergence of a New Automobile Hub in Europe
The Offensive Strategies of the Principal Manufacturers are of a Pan-European Nature
No Major Upheaval in the European Automobile Market, but a Challenge

5. India and EU Enlargement: Challenges and Opportunities **153**
Economic Implications of EU Enlargement
EU Enlargement and its Impact on India-EU Trade Linkages
EU Enlargement and its Impact on India-EU Investment Linkages
Analysis of the Keys Sectors
India and the New Europe: Issues and Challenges
Recommendations

References **171**

Index **173**

List of Tables and Figures

TABLES

1.1 The New Economic and Institutional Europe (EU27) After the Nice Treaty 15

1.2 Accession Negociations: State of Play in December 2000 24

1.3 Financial Assistance for New Members, Indicative Programming 2000-06 28

1.4 Growth, GDP and Forecast of Convergence between the EU15 and the 12 New Member States 40

2.1 FDI Performance Index 1998-2000 53

2.2 Stock of FDI in CEECs 64

2.3 FDI Potential of Progress with or without EU Membership 65

2.4 Sectoral Breakdown of FDI in CEECs (Per cent Total Stock) 71

2.5 Households Disposal of Consumer Durable Goods in CEECs, France and Portugal 80

3.1 Trade Opening Intensity for CEECs (Export+Import)/ GDP at Current Exchange Rate) 85

3.2 The New Geographical Trade Patterns of CEECs 1992-2000 88

3.3 The Intra-CEE Trade Dynamism 92

3.4 Evolution of the CEECs in the EU and French Total Import from the World 108

4.1 CEECs in the French Textiles Trade between 1990 and 2000 122

5.1 Estimated Simple Average MFN Applied Tariffs (ACs & EU) in Percentage 155

5.2 IT Services Spending: Regional Shares, 2002-03 160

5.3 Comparative Cost between Europe and India in Pharmaceuticals 161

5.4 Problems Faced by Indian Companies Exporting to the Central & East European Countries 163

5.5 Brief Summary of Accession Countries 166

FIGURES

2.1 Index of Unit Labour Cost (UE15=100) in 1999 54

2.2 EU15 Outward FDI flows (Bn €) 59

3.1 Trade Flows and GDP Indexes During the Post-communist Transition (100 in 1990) 86

4.1 CEECs Share in the World and EU Import of Textiles (garment included)

World Import 119

EU15 Import 119

4.2 Evolution of the Furniture Trade from CEE 1995-2000 129

4.3 Evolution of the CEECs' Share in the EU27 Supply and Demand for Car in 2000 and 2010 (estimtes) 146

4.4 Trade between France and CEECs in the Automotive Sector 1991-2002 149

5.1 India's Exports to the EU in 2002-03: Country-wise Distribution 152

5.2 India's Imports from EU in 2002-03: Country-wise Distribution 152

5.3 India's Exports to Accession Countries ('02-'03): Country-wise Distribution 153

5.4 India's Imports from Accession Countries ('02-'03): Country-wise Distribution 153

5.5 FDI into India from EU from 1991 to 2003: Country-wise Distribution 157

5.6 FDI into India from Accession Countries from 1991 to 2003 Country-wise Distribution 157

European Union's map of Europe

▭	European Union EU Member States
▭	Candidate Countries
▭	Non-member Countries

© *European Commission*

Introduction

The enlargement of the European Union (EU) to 25 members in May 2004, and probably between 32 to 37 in the next decade will not unduly change the place of Europe in the world economy. For instance despite the high growth potential, estimated at 4 to 5 per cent per annum, as against 2 to 2.5 per cent for the existing 15 members, the 12 central and eastern Europe countries by 2010, will account for, at best, only 11 per cent of the Greater EU's GDP as against 8.5 per cent in 2000 (in terms of purchasing power parity).

The issues at stake in the new economic geography will, on the other hand, prove to be much more significant. As a matter of fact, the entry of these countries is the culmination of an intense process of economic integration of the satellite countries of the former USSR, which widens the cost matrix of production within which European firms are operating, while also expanding the market matrix through which firms can sell within the EU. This constitutes a formidable new order not only for all the European companies, but also for those that wish to establish themselves in Europe or those that have to face competition from firms operating within a Greater Europe.

From a global perspective, this can have important consequences. First, Europe is not entrenched in its 'fortress'; there are objective factors for a partial re-routing of business traffic since all the surveys on competitiveness show the strong attraction held by the east European economies. The last Kearney report, which placed India and China at the top of the list, included also the three major east European economies among the 10 most attractive countries of the world.

Actually, in the last few years, the flow of foreign direct investment towards east Europe has been so massive that a small country like the Czech Republic (which has a population of only 10 million) attracts more foreign direct investment (FDI) than the whole of India ($8 billion in 2003). The major share of these FDI comes from the 'old' European economies such as Germany and France.

Second, the enlargement of the EU will lead to political, institutional and economic restructuring. This critical phase will persist for at least a decade, during which Europe may be more preoccupied with its own unification problems. From this point of view, the possibility of Europe becoming a global force capable of taking on the American economy is not off the mark, but it will be many years before it can become a practical reality.

On the other hand, there is no question that the enlarged Europe is becoming virtually the world's largest economy, with its 450- to 550-million inhabitants, if we include all the new countries that will be sharing the economic space of Greater Europe, whether or not they are officially members of the EU, such as Turkey.

This means that we must strive to fully understand the new geographical trends in the European economy. The latter is less and less a collection of countries and ever more a space centred around new economic regions that goes beyond the old national frontiers, a bit like the situation existing in the American economy.

Indeed, one of the consequences of the expansion towards the east is the restructuring of the European economic space into five belts or zones, within which business transactions will probably be reinforced: north Europe (the old nucleus of the EU 15), the Baltic Rim, central Europe, South-eastern Europe, and lastly, the Iberian zone.

These are clear indications of a more polymorphous space, more fragmented somehow than the largely mono-centred Europe that existed around the famous London-Franche-Comte-Hamburg triangle, and represented 55 per cent of the nominal GDP of the old EU15, a third of its population and one-seventh of its area.

These large areas do not really correspond to national frontiers but rather to regional spaces characterised by:

- Strong historical links, just like the ancient Hanseatic league around the Baltic Sea, with similar consumption habits and industrial cultures.
- Much greater intensity of exchanges and investment among the hubs than with other EU countries and, therefore,

presenting an additional advantage to the firms directly present in these hubs.

- Greater specialisation of labour within these hubs, of the horizontal intra-industry type between developed regions such as Germany, but henceforth, also vertical with the entry of the less-developed new members.

At the same time, we see a growing sectorial specialisation in these emerging new regions, although without attaining the levels of the famous large belts of the US. For example, Seattle specialises in the aeronautical industry, and the Great Lakes region in the automobile industry. In the enlarged Europe, a new electronic belt is emerging in the Baltic Rim, one for the automotive industry in central Europe (including south Germany), and another one for the apparel industry in the eastern zone, which Italy and even Turkey have taken full advantage of in the past few years.

All this re-organisation of the European productive space will, of course, take decades to complete. But it is nevertheless imperative for companies to reposition themselves now in view of the significant changes that will take place in the medium term. As for those selling in the European markets, they must understand that the European competitiveness is discovering new internal sources that the more developed European countries may have previously lost. And they have also to adapt their commercial network and marketing strategy to the new economic geography of Europe. But the challenge goes beyond. For decision makers, for professors, for students, the new making of Europe in the coming decades is increasingly become part of the understanding of the future global economy in which India will inevitably play a growing role.

New powers like India and China will...

1

The Institutional and Economic Rationale Behind Enlargement

Institutional Rationality: The EU Methodology

The success of the ongoing enlargement process depends mainly on the respect of the Union methodology. It involves a long and slow process of periodic consultations, intermediary goals, a consensual will and above all pragmatism. The different stages of the current enlargement as well as the tools employed since 1990 are a testimony to this.[1]

From Copenhagen (June 1993) to Copenhagen (December 2002)

The process of enlargement to all intents and purposes was initiated during the June 1993 Copenhagen European Council. Mainly, the principles and rules of negotiation were spelt out at this juncture. The 15 Member States took an historical decision to include the Central and East European countries in the European Union, whose eligibility would be judged on the basis of three criteria, which would remain valid for all future memberships, and would henceforth be known as the Copenhagen criteria. Thus, to join the European Union, candidate countries must ensure:

- the 'stability of institutions guaranteeing democracy, the rule of law, human rights and the respect for and protection of minorities';
- 'the existence of a functioning market economy as well as the capacity to cope with competitive pressure and market forces with the Union';

---

1. An excellent expose of the method can be found in the brochure published and regularly updated by the Commission: The Enlargement of the European Union, an historical opportunity, accessible on the website: http://Europa.eu.int/comm/enlargement/.

- 'ability to take on the obligations of membership, including adherence to the aims of political, economic and monetary union'.

At a more formal level a new parameter, the *acquis communautaire*, was developed for all Member States to follow.

The Luxembourg European Council, held in December 1997, marked the effective beginning of the negotiation process. The member states decided that membership negotiations would be opened in March 1998, with the six countries at the time considered as the most closely adhering to the Copenhagen criteria: Cyprus, Estonia, Hungary, Poland, Czech Republic and Slovenia. The six other candidate countries were not considered sufficiently advanced in a certain number of sectors, especially the economic, but to some extent the political also. The member states moreover wished that the accession process be founded on a simple principle : namely differentiation, according to which each country would advance in the negotiations in keeping with the progress effectively realised. This would come to be known as the famous Regata principle, to borrow a yachting term. Lastly, to help countries to prepare for membership, the EU launched a sustained pre-accession strategy for the benefit of the ten CEEC candidates, which mobilised nearly 3 billion Euros per annum.

In December 1999, the Helsinki European Council, marked the extension of the process. Negotiations were opened with the six candidate countries that had not been retained earlier : Bulgaria, Latvia, Lithuania, Malta, Romania and Slovakia. At the same time, Turkey was also recognized as a candidate country without, however, the accession negotiations being engaged, especially as the political criteria had not been met.

The Nice European Council of December 2000, under French presidency, set the tempo for the negotiations. It ended on a dual acceleration factor for the enlargement of the Union : firstly, the proposal of a road map 2000-2002 to assist in the completion of the negotiations and, secondly, an institutional compromise allowing the entry of twelve new member countries into the EU, i.e. an unequivocal political commitment with regard to the irreversibility of the process (Table 1.1).

Table 1.1

The New Economic and Institutional Europe (EU27) After the Nice Treaty

Pays	Population Millions	Votes at the Council	Seats at the European Parliament	GDP Bn USD	Population Millions	Votes at the Council	Seats at the European Parliament	GDP Bn USD
	Numbers				in Per cent UE27			
	Old Members States							
Germany	82.1	29	99	1737	17.1	8	14	20.5
Austria	8.1	10	17	178	1.7	3	2	2.1
Belgium	10.2	12	22	235	2.1	3	3	2.8
Denmark	5.3	7	13	122	1.1	2	2	1.4
Spain	39.4	27	50	617	8.2	8	7	7.3
Finland	5.2	7	13	116	1.1	2	2	1.4
France	58.5	29	72	1301	12.2	8	10	15.4
Greece	10.5	12	22	132	2.2	3	3	1.6
Irland	3.7	7	12	81	0.8	2	2	1.0
Italy	57.6	29	72	1156	12.0	8	10	13.6
Luxemburg	0.4	4	6	14	0.1	1	1	0.2
Pays-Bas	15.8	13	25	332	3.3	4	3	3.9
Portugal	10	12	22	141	2.1	3	3	1.7
U.K.	59.2	29	72	1222	12.3	8	10	14.4
Sweden	8.9	10	18	168	1.9	3	2	2.0

Contd...

...Table 1.1 Contd...

Pays	*Population Millions*	*Votes at the Council*	*Seats at the European Parliament*	*GDP Bn USD*	*Population Millions*	*Votes at the Council*	*Seats at the European Parliament*	*GDP Bn USD*
	Numbers				*in Per cent UE27*			
	New Members and Candidates Countries							
Bulgaria*	8.3	10	17	43	1.7	3	2	0.5
Cyprus	0.8	4	6	11	0.2	1	1	0.1
Estonia	1.4	4	6	12	0.3	1	1	0.1
Hungary	10.1	12	20	114	2.1	3	3	1.3
Latvia	2.4	4	8	15	0.5	1	1	0.2
Lithuania	3.7	7	12	25	0.8	2	2	0.3
Malta	0.4	3	5	6	0.1	1	1	0.1
Poland	38.7	27	50	342	8.0	8	7	4.0
Romania*	22.4	14	33	130	4.7	4	5	1.5
Slovakia	5.4	7	13	55	1.1	2	2	0.6
Slovenia	2	4	7	31	0.4	1	1	0.4
Czech R.	10.3	12	20	138	2.1	3	3	1.6
Total	**480.8**	**345**	**732**	**8474**	100.0	100	100	100.0

* will join after 2007 or 2008.

Source: EU Commission.

On the first point, the time table proposed was based on the actual progress of the candidate countries. In its Regular Report on the progress made by these countries, during the Nice European Council the European Commission presented an overall highly satisfactory outcome with regard to the accession criteria fixed in Copenhagen in June 1993. A roadmap was drawn on the basis of the results to steer the accession negotiations during 2000-2002. The aim was to complete them *de facto* in time for the Copenhagen European Council of December 2002, a symbolic date as the process had come full circle a decade after its launching in the very same Danish capital.

Since 1997, each year the Commission analyses the progress of the candidate countries with regard to the accession criteria fixed at Copenhagen. The 2000 report presented at Nice posted a globally satisfying picture, although there were marked differences between the candidate countries. The outcome with regard to Cyprus and Malta was thus very positive and it was favourable for Hungary, Poland and Estonia. There were some grey areas where the Czech Republic and Slovenia were concerned, and it was uneven in the case of Slovakia, Lithuania and Latvia. On the other hand it was not so favourable for Bulgaria and even less for Romania. It was clear that there would be an initial rush of accessions involving ten countries, while a date, around 2007, was set for the two less advanced states. Officially, of course, no date was formally retained, in conformity with the 1992 policy, and the principle thereof by which a certain number of conditions had to be fulfilled in order to be accepted as a member of the Union.

At Nice, the Commission proposed a rather effective method to deal with the 'sticky points' of the negotiations. In view of the increasingly frequent requests for special dispensation and transitional periods for the adoption of the *acquis*, a more rigorous treatment was proposed. Of course, some members conceded that in relation to certain sensitive sectors, such as environment, this was not a very realistic prerequisite to accession.

Over and above its technical aspects, the handling of the transitional periods demanded by the candidate countries, gave rise to some important economic, budgetary and trade issues. The respect for the rules of competition common to all countries is at stake. On the other hand, the transitory periods have some legitimate relevance in fields necessitating a particularly important financial effort such as environment, energy and infrastructure. The great danger is, however, to find transitory periods accumulating. More than 450 such requests were thus submitted to the European Commission during the Nice European Council. Hence, the latter had to specify the condition of admissibility. To be admissible, the transitional periods must be limited in time and in scope; be accompanied by a plan with a well-defined agenda for the adoption of the *acquis*; must not bring major distortions in their wake arising from competitiveness; and lastly, must be brief and few in fields related to the extension of the single market.

Second breakthrough at Nice : although often criticised and placed in an awkward position judicially by the Irish 'NO' during its referendum in 2001,[2] an institutional agreement was arrived at among the 15 with regard to a large part of the institutional architecture of a 27-strong Europe – and especially the new vote balance in the European Council and the Parliament. The compromise, which was only reached after a great deal of discussion, was a notable success for enlargement. Of course, there were the usual frustrations inherent in all exercises of this type, and more so when it meant irreversibly laying down the norms underlying the distribution of votes in the principal institutions of European power. The sense of compromise does not, however, facilitate decision-making on some crucial aspects of the functioning of the institutions, in particular, the number of the commissioners from each country and on the manner of functioning of the reinforced cooperation groups. As we can see, there is a plethora of reforms on which the European Convention on the future of the EU is currently working, a decision taken at Nice to perfect before 2004, whatever has not been completed.

The Laeken European Council of December 2001, ushered in the final phase of the negotiations. Ignored for a long time, the idea of drawing up a timetable for accessions gradually took shape under pressure from the candidate countries. The European Council thus adopted the scenario known as the 'big-bang' in favour of the simultaneous accession of the largest number of countries

2. Nevertheless, the Irish voters massively approved (62.9 per cent) the Treaty of Nice in the second referendum on October 19, 2002.

considered to be in a position to conclude the negotiations by the end of 2002, so that they could participate in the European parliamentary election as full members of the EU in 2004. For the first time, the conclusions drawn at Laeken listed the ten countries that could eventually form part of the initial wave of accessions, including in effect Poland and explicitly excluding Romania, Bulgaria and - a special case - Turkey. They confirmed that henceforth the political dimension would have greater importance as compared to the technical dimension of the process. For all that, the Spanish and later the Danish presidencies for the two 2002 semesters inherited an explosive road map, especially the agricultural and budgetary chapters, which it had been decided would be taken up towards the end of the negotiations, another tradition in the EU methodology which has proved itself. The unfortunate configuration of the political cycle in Europe nevertheless considerably obstructed political arbitration, which was always prepared in advance. As for example, the Dutch elections in March, which exhibited a hardening on the part of a section of European public opinion in view of the increasingly supranational decisions (in fact quasi federal by nature) being taken; after that French elections in late spring, and German in autumn, countries seen as the two great protagonists of a possible compromise at the Copenhagen European Council. In fact it is these dates that set the tempo of the last few weeks of negotiation. Some days prior to the Brussels European Council on the 26th and 27th October, 2002, a Franco-German agreement, negotiated directly between President Chirac and Chancellor Schroeder, opened the way for a vital compromise on the agricultural and budgetary chapters. The granting of direct aid to farmers in the new member countries was retained in exchange for a ceiling on market expenditure and direct payments by the Union for the period 2004-2013 at the level of 2006, and increased by 1 per cent per year. Direct aid to candidate countries is limited to 25 per cent of the EU15 level in the first year (2004), then 30 per cent in the next year, till parity is gradually reached by 2013.

Broadly speaking, the financial agreement in view of enlargement has allocated a Budget of 39.3 billion Euros for the period 2004-2006, corresponding to the completion of the Berlin budgetary cycle, of which 23 billion are earmarked as pre-accession aid for structural programmes.

Lastly, the Brussels Council confirmed the ten countries retained in the first enlargement of 2004, made a small gesture in support of the 2007 objective regarding Bulgaria and Romania and satisfied itself by declaring that 'the political and economic progress realised by Turkey indicates that the prospect of opening the accession negotiations is closer.' But in response to the anxieties of some member states, the Brussels Council also stiffened the conditions for monitoring the implementation of the *acquis communautaire* by the member countries. In addition to the Commission's publication of a new 'Follow-up Report' before the accession date, the Council approved the inclusion of a *general economic safety clause* and *two specific clauses*. The first, relating to the functioning of the internal market, the second in the field of the Justice and Home Affairs (JHA), could be implemented on the basis of an 'imminent risk' and invoked only by the current member states during a period of three years after accession.

The few weeks separating Brussels from the historic Copenhagen Council of December 14, 2002, were particularly charged as negotiations on some rather sensitive points raised by candidate countries in the last phase of bargaining became very heated. This entailed mainly government aid to specific industries, such as mining, on which a report published in early December stated that on an average it exceeded the relative EU15level. But in general, firmness prevailed, if only because of the growing concern for the respect by all of the rules governing a single market, and secondly, to avoid laying oneself open to criticism over delocalisation, which received a shot in the arm because of dumping by the candidate countries.

The Copenhagen Council could now ratify the fourth historic enlargement of the European Union, probably the most symbolic in political terms, but also the largest in absolute terms of area and population (75 million people from ten countries). Although 2007 was maintained as the accession date for Bulgaria and Romania, in Turkey's case, however, there was a heated debate, instigated by the President of the Convention, Valéry Giscard d'Estaing, some weeks earlier. In spite of the Turkish leader, Recep Tayyip Erdogan's highly publicised European tour, the Council refused to commit itself to a date for the accession negotiations with Turkey and was content with the drafting of a rendezvous clause.

The schedule for next few months was heavy : completion of the draft of the accession treaty by Spring 2003; signing of this treaty in April of the same year; followed by ratification procedures of the treaty lasting close to a year, namely through referendums in all the member countries, which could bring some unexpected surprises; and finally, May 2004, if all went well, accession would come into force, which would be followed by full-scale participation in the European parliamentary elections of June 2004.

At the same time, the work of the Convention was normally supposed to end by Spring 2003 and an inter-governmental Conference held towards the close of 2003. This was slated to open the way for a new fundamental treaty leading to a revivified European Union largely restructured on the basis of political and institutional plans. This would thus be the end of the eastern enlargement-refinement cycle, historically inaugurated after the fall of the Berlin Wall in November 1989. Something no one could foresee was the extent to which it would change the face of Europe in the span of a decade the stalemate after the French and Dutch popular rejection of the proposed Constitution in 2005 only means that the Nice treaty remains the legal framework for the entire EU.

The Four Pillars of the Enlargement Process

As with all European history, the time factor, the institutional processes founded on tried and tested juridical rules and often sustained by an underlying pragmatism, and lastly, the well-calculated financial doses, constitute the three ingredients of the Community methodology. The four pillars of the current process of enlargement once again bear testimony to this.

The Association Agreements (or the European Agreements)

The Association Agreements (or European Agreements) signed between the Union and each candidate country, constitute a first essential step towards accession. For the most part concluded in the first half of the nineties, they comprise a triple dimension - political, commercial and economic - which provides the juridical basis for the piecemeal re-unification process between the two parts of Europe, separated since the end of the Second World War. The former

Democratic German Republic cannot be taken as a prototype, both juridically as well politically and economically.

The commercial dimension especially played a decisive role in the initial stages of the break from communism because of the support it provided for the re-orientation of trade flows, one of the keys to the success of economic transition. In particular, it organised the gradual and asymmetrical opening of a free trade zone enabling a very rapid re-orientation of trade towards the Western countries, aiming to compensate the breakdown of flows between the Comecon countries.[3] Thus, the Union removed the quantitative restrictions and customs duty on all industrial products from the candidate countries and accorded them working rights prevailing in the country in the area of services.[4] The candidate countries, rather sensitive to competitive pressure, had the advantage of more flexible arrangements enabling them to maintain restrictions on the trade of goods (until 2001, and even 2003 in the case of some products such as cars) and services (2004). Agricultural products are given special treatment because agriculture constitutes an extremely sensitive issue on both sides of the Berlin Wall.

The powerful trade fallout that followed played a major role in compensating for the terrible shock of transition, as we shall see in chapter 3.

The Negotiations Framework: The 31 Chapters of the *'Acquis Communautaire'*

The European Council, very early on, laid down the broad guidelines for negotiation : the *acquis communautaire* must be adopted and effectively applied; the transitory period must be of limited

3. The Council for Mutual Economic Assistance (Comecon), created in 1949 by the USSR, is an organisation of economic cooperation between socialist countries for the purpose of coordinating and facilitating the reconstruction and development of these countries and promoting trade between them. It included Bulgaria, Hungary, Poland, Czechoslovakia, Romania, Mongolia, USSR, Cuba (since 1972) and Vietnam (since 1978). United Germany has assumed the international commitments undertaken by East Germany, a founding member of Comecon. In early 1991, trade which till now had been based on a fixed rouble or by barter, is done in convertible currency, also customs duty between members of the organisation is introduced. Comecon was dissolved on June 28, 1991.
4. Which enabled citizens of the candidate countries to legally take a job in the services sector in the EU15 countries, on condition that they satisfied the legislation in force.

duration and scope, and accompanied by a timetable for the adoption of the *acquis*; the pace of negotiations with each country must take into account, on the basis of the differentiation principle, the progress actually achieved; and lastly, there cannot be a definite partial agreement without a global agreement.

This negotiation presented the European Union with an opportunity to take stock of the *acquis*, i.e. whether or not it was being effectively applied by the 15 Member States (France itself has been late in regard to some chapters such as the liberalisation of the energy sector). Divided into 31 chapters (see Table 1.2), which in the year 2000 covered not less than 80000 pages of EU legislation, and to which several hundred more are added every year. A Herculean task for the candidate countries, which would result in specific assistance being provided such as administrative twinning and also lead to necessary compromises by which the more financially burdensome measures would be staggered over a period (sanitary norms and water, for example). Overall, 372 chapters are negotiated by the twelve candidates, a formidable task on the face of it. For a long time it was feared that the enlargement process with the East European countries would take more than 10 years to complete. This was not the case, despite the meticulous examination, chapter by chapter, of the provisions by the candidate countries. This can be explained by a combination of the strong political will motivating the candidates, and the painstaking work by the Commission as well as the 15 national delegations responsible for the follow up of the negotiations, under the responsibility of the respective foreign affairs ministries.

In concrete terms, the negotiations with the Luxembourg six (Cyprus, Estonia, Hungary, Poland Czech Republic and Slovenia) commenced only in March 1998. The negotiations with the Helsinki six (Bulgaria, Latvia, Lithuania, Malta, Romania and Slovakia), for their part began as late as February 2000, but were marked with such a strong urge to catch up that within a few months it became difficult to distinguish between the two groups. Some countries such as the Baltic States and also Slovakia even outstripped the countries of the first group in terms of the number of chapters closed. However, some chapters gave rise to serious difficulties and at times negotiations became strained.

Table 1.2

Accession Negociations: State of Play in December 2000

No.	CHAPTER	CYP	CZECH	EST	HUN	POL	SLO	BUL	LAT	LIT	MAL	ROM	SLK
1	Free movement of goods	X	X	X	0	0	0	~	~	~	~	~	~
2	Free movement of persons	0	0	0	0	0	0	~	~	~	~	~	~
3	Free movement of services	0	0	0	0	X	X	~	0	0	~	~	0
4	Free movement of capital	0	0	X	0	0	0	0	0	0	0	~	0
5	Company law	X	0	X	0	0	X	0	0	0	X	~	~
6	Competition	0	0	0	0	0	0	~	0	0	0	0	0
7	Agriculture	0	0	0	0	0	0	~	~	~	~	~	~
8	Fisheries	X	X	X	X	0	X	~	0	~	0	~	X
9	Transport	0	0	0	0	0	0	~	0	0	0	~	0
10	Taxation	0	0	0	0	0	0	~	~	~	~	~	~
11	EMU	X	X	X	X	X	X	~	X	~	X	~	~
12	Statistics	X	X	X	X	X	X	X	X	X	X	X	X
13	Social policy	X	0	X	X	0	X	~	~	0	0	~	~
14	Energy	0	0	0	X	0	0	~	~	~	~	~	~
15	Industry	X	X	X	X	X	X	~	X	X	X	~	X
16	SMEs	X	X	X	X	X	X	X	X	X	X	X	X
17	Science and research	X	X	X	X	X	X	X	X	X	X	X	X
18	Education and training	X	X	X	X	X	X	X	X	X	X	X	X

Contd...

...Contd...

No.	CHAPTER	CYP	CZECH	EST	HUN	POL	SLO	BUL	LAT	LIT	MAL	ROM	SLK
19	Telecommunication	X	X	X	X	X	X	0	~	0	X	0	0
20	Culture and audiovisual	X	0	X	0	X	0	X	0	0	X	0	X
21	Regional policy	0	0	0	0	0	0	~	~	~	~	~	~
22	Environment	0	0	0	0	0	0	~	~	0	~	~	~
23	Consumers and health protection	X	X	X	X	X	X	X	X	~	X	~	X
24	Justice and home affairs	0	0	0	0	0	0	~	~	~	~	~	~
25	Customs union	X	X	0	0	0	0	~	~	~	~	~	0
26	External relations	X	X	X	X	X	0	X	X	X	X	X	X
27	CFSP	X	X	X	X	X	X	X	X	X	X	X	X
28	Financial control	X	0	0	X	X	X	~	~	~	~	~	~
29	Financial and budgetary provisions	0	0	0	0	0	0	~	~	~	~	~	~
30	Institutions												
	Chapters opened	29	29	29	29	29	29	11	16	16	17	9	16

0: Chapter opened, under negotiation.

X: Chapter provisionally closed.

~: Chapter not yet opened to negotiation.

Source: European Commission, December 2000.

In the first phase of the negotiations, in which the more sensitive chapters were deliberately not opened, those chapters which presented the most problems dealt with issues relating to the single market[5] and to certain politically sensitive common policies; or else they necessitated heavy investments (audiovisual, energy, transport, taxation, environment). After a short period of adaptation and putting in place teams of well-trained negotiators, the candidate countries fiercely defended their interests and increased their requests for transitional measures or amendments. By the end of 2000, the six Luxembourg countries alone had submitted more than 380 demands, which explains why such stringent norms (see supra) were adopted at Nice. One of the more difficult issues in the first set of chapters was the liberalisation of land acquisition, especially in Poland but also in Hungary. Both were concerned about the disparities in purchasing power on the two sides of their Western border. They therefore demanded 15 and 10 years respectively before foreigners were permitted to buy agricultural property in their country. A compromise was finally reached – 7 years – but it was not easy.

Much more delicate were the chapters on agriculture, regional policy, free circulation of individuals and budgetary issues, which were opened for negotiations only in June 2000. When the stakes were financial or affected the interests of the member states themselves, the points of friction sometimes blocked the negotiations. This was the case with the chapter 'free circulation of individuals', behind which lay the migration issue. Public opinion in some cases, especially in the neighbouring countries, openly manifested its anxiety and wished to open up very gradually, following the example of the three south European countries, Spain, Portugal and Greece. The final compromise adopted the enlargement precedent set in the eighties, but allowing greater flexibility to the Member State, both in terms of execution and criteria for qualification.

With regard to the agricultural and budgetary questions, to find a common position among the 15 countries was like walking a

5. Such as company law, external relations, free circulation of capital, services and goods, or customs union.

tightrope, in view of the tension generated at the time of the adoption of the 1999-2000 budget at Berlin. This time 12 much poorer countries, in comparison to the European Union average, had to be taken into account. Thus, by definition they were potential beneficiaries of positive net transfers to the detriment of the rich countries, that is to say some of the erstwhile poor countries, such as Ireland and Spain.

The Process of Financial Support: The EU Programmes

The grand European unification project takes the form of various community aid programmes, often criticised for their defects. However, without them the attempt at unification would remain an empty shell. With 3 billion Euros per annum even before accession, and three to four times more after it, their aim was to provide leverage through transfers of technologies, whether originating from governments or firms. Once the institutional mechanisms were integrated and tested, thanks to the initial assistance programmes, the purely financial aspects would play a much more important role, as they would amount to 3 to 4 per cent of the GDP of the new members, as in the case of Spain and Portugal in the years 1985-1995.

Is this process effective? Undoubtedly, both for the civil services of the candidate countries as well as for the private firms, that adapted themselves in the face of the cumbersome 'continental' procedures in every sense of the term. There is no lack of positive examples, like the small industry from the Lyon region, which opened a mini state-of-the-art garbage treatment plant near Budapest airport some years ago, whose technology is much in demand by environment giants. The increasing use of the Internet is worth highlighting here. We can henceforth find all the details of the pre-accession programmes on the DG Enlargement website[6]. The failures are probably just as many but receive much more publicity, such as the scandals in Poland and Romania during 2002[7].

6. http://Europa.eu.int/comm/enlargement
7. In the summer of 2002, the Polish and Romanian authorities were ordered to reimburse large sums money of European origin, which had been diverted from their intended use.

Table 1.3

Financial Assistance for New Members, Indicative Programming 2000-06

	TOTAL		*PHARE*	*ISPA*		*SAPARD*
	Minim.	*Maxim.*	*Average/Year*	*Minim.*	*Maxim.*	*Average/Year*
Bulgaria	235	277	100	83	125	52
Czech R.	158	184	79	57	83	22
Estonia	57	73	24	21	36	12
Hungary	207	238	96	73	104	38
Latvia	88	109	30	36	57	22
Lithuania	113	134	42	42	62	30
Poland	879	952	398	312	385	169
Romania	601	663	242	208	270	151
Slovakia	104	125	49	36	57	18
Slovenia	42	52	25	10	21	6
TOTAL	2484	2806	1485*	879	1201	520

Source: Agenda 2000, European Commission, Million of Euros.

In budgetary terms, the annual monetary mass represents a little more than 3 billion Euros for the period 2000-2006, apportioned in the following manner : 1.6 billion for PHARE, 1 billion for ISPA and 520 million for SAPARD. The indicative annual allocations for 2000-2006 are shown in Table 1.3. The beneficiaries are mainly : administrative bodies on the institutional side (twinning in particular); consultants and engineering firms; and firms supplying products for projects. These organisations must belong to one of the member states of the EU or a beneficiary country. In terms of programming, the Accession Partnerships (AP) and the National Programmes for the Adoption of the *Acquis* (NPAA) form the general and pluri-annual framework of the three instruments of pre-accession. Moreover, each candidate country has to formulate its sectoral strategy through a National Development Plan (NDP), a Rural Development Plan (RDP) and strategic documents in the sectors of transport and environment. The accession partnerships are further refined by the National Development Plans, which indicate the priority sectors; the Rural Development Plan, required by SAPARD, and lastly, the strategy documents relating to transport and environment, required by ISPA. If the procedures appear cumbersome, and they probably are, their pedagogic and structuralistic character on the institutional front cannot be ignored. It is not possible to make the transition from centrally planned economies, in other words authoritarian, to an efficient mixed economy without an apprenticeship of this kind.

In order to take into account the progress of the accession process and reinforce the responsibility of the partnership countries, the Commission has given a new orientation to PHARE since 2002 : pluri-annual programming; the move towards decentralisation of EU delegatons, lastly, the introduction of an intra-community approach, especially with reference to Structural Funds pertaining to the economic and social cohesion programmes.

A Process of Institutional Support: The Reinforcement of the Administrative Capacities

The reinforcement of the administrative capacities to adopt the *acquis* was gradually confirmed as the EU priority as and when accessions approached. The enlargement of the EU constitutes a promising framework for all concerned on the condition that the process remains under control. The Commission and the Member States are fully aware that the commitments undertaken will have to be very closely monitored so that they do not remain merely on paper. They have, therefore, progressively introduced a new priority for the candidate countries : close monitoring of the progress effectively achieved in the adoption of the *acquis communautaire*. In 2002, this plan was given top priority, accompanied by the redeployment of the PHARE funds, the main beneficiary of which is twinning between the administrations of the member states and that of the applicant countries. Lastly, as when the first accessions in 2004 began to take shape, discussions ensued over the sanctions (especially financial) to be imposed in order to prevent defaulting on commitments.

The reinforcement of the administrative capacity especially focuses on four priorities : the functioning of the domestic market (existence of an appropriate regulatory authority in the fields of competition, telecommunication, energy and transport....); sustainable development in the EU (environmental norms, high level of nuclear security, improvement in transport safety; the safety of citizens (observance of sanitary norms, food security, cooperation in the field of justice and home affairs....); and lastly, the management of the community funds which necessitate appropriate structures in the regional and central governments to ensure the implementation of the rules governing procurement contracts, financial control, audit as well as the prevention of fraud and corruption.

In exchange for financial aid and compliance with the programmes by each candidate country, *ad hoc* peer reviews were recently introduced. Experts from the Member States and the Commission analyse the administrative capacities of the applicant countries. Six sectors were specially targeted : financial services, justice and home affairs, budgetary issues, agriculture, nuclear security and environment. These reviews are essential as they facilitate the monitoring of commitments. In addition to compliance with and the disappearance of these joint programmes, discussions took place on the introduction of realistic sanctions in case the commitments with regard to the *acquis communautaire* were not respected (see supra, safety clauses).

We can see that in the mid-nineties the profound transformation of the Eastern economies was marked by the institutional process of the transfer of West European norms, confirming that development is above all an institutional matter. It is not by a 'big-bang' that they are built, but by a conscious and steady effort at adaptation over the long term. Starting with the hypothesis that the community methodology has until now largely borne its fruit in terms of the pace of institutional change in the 12 candidate countries, the micro and macro-economic importance of this enlargement for the whole of Europe is examined in the following chapters.

Economic Rationality: A Twin Gain for Europe

Ensuring the Success of the Post-communist Transition

The rapidity with which the European continent achieved re-unification has frequently resulted in erasing from memory the condition of the eastern economies during the transition after the collapse of the communist bloc. To recapitulate: the drop in economic activity by half, and in some cases more; signs of hyper-inflation everywhere; complete disruption of trade; and serious concerns about the capacity of the various populations to bear the shock. The image of Warsaw with its near-empty State-owned shops in the spring of 1990, a phenomenon that gradually spread to nearly all the vulnerable countries in the zone, had indeed disappeared from public memories ten years later.

Actually, this is probably true of the younger generation, but not of those who have now retired, most of whom had to live with the shame of near-destitution for many years. The shock of the new reality in the post-communist era, after the fall of the Berlin Wall, was very great, and not only in ex-USSR but also in Central and Eastern Europe. Some specialists, and highly respected ones at that, are of the opinion that several generations would be needed to reconstruct the post-communist economies, not to mention the fears of political and social instability in a historically fragile region. The Yugoslavian crisis is a good illustration of the disasters that an uncontrolled rupture can bring about.

However, ten, almost fifteen years down the line, the post-communist transition in Central and Eastern Europe appears to be an overall success. Probably because the radical method recommended by one of the greatest Hungarian economists, Jànos Kornaï,[8] proved the most effective. But also to a great extent because Eastern Europe outside ex-USSR was able to profit immediately from a powerful push-pull effect due to the European Union. It is from this very phenomenon that Romania and Bulgaria began to benefit at this time, the two countries of the region that were most affected by the authoritarian political system. The current trends in the western Balkans offer the same glimmer of hope with the first concerted steps taken in 1998 for accession to the EU.

Success is gauged not so much by the standard of living measured in terms of official GDP figures alone, much of which was artificial in the planned economic system, than by the quality of economic institutions set up, which the European Bank for Reconstruction and Development (EBRD) has been evaluating regularly since 1991. Even if the institutions are not up to the mark in some cases and even if

---

8. This writer of Hungarian origin, recommended as early as 1990 in his book cum programme, From Socialism to Capitalism. The Hungarian example, to put into application as quickly as possible, the basic market reforms and rigorous programmes for macro-economic stabilisation in order to prevent a hyper-inflationist crisis. His advices were widely followed, although it was mixed with a gradualist approach in various spheres, in particular trade and institutional changes.

they need time to evolve, their net improvement, according to the projections of most experts, can lead to a steady economic recovery of about 4 per cent to 5 per cent per annum. The performances are so much the more remarkable as we are dealing with averages, behind which are concealed sectors still in the process of restructuring while others have achieved double digit growth, as the former director general of the IMF, Jacques de Larosiere judiciously remarked during a regional conference in Budapest, in June 2001. So much the more remarkable also because the pace of this growth in per capita terms, places the central European transition economies up among the leaders of the emerging economies of the world, as the Bank for International Settlements (BIS) noted in its report in the summer of 2002.

Proof of the efficacy of the commitment to European enlargement immediately after the collapse of the Soviet bloc is gauged clearly from the fact that transition was all the more successful as the concerned countries had a common border with the European Union. In particular the Association Agreements (see *infra*) signed at the outset of the transition process, enabled the rapid liberalisation of trade and direct investments. Once more, the adage *Trade Not Aid* was vindicated. Indeed, the economic reunification of Europe began well before its institutional reunification.

Firstly, with the free movement of persons, even if its economic effects are not very obvious. Since 1990, several hundred thousand workers have found employment in Western Europe during the most difficult stage of transition. According to the data collected by the German Institute DIW,[9] the European Union in 1998 officially accounted for a little more than 850,000 people from the ten Central and East European countries. If we take into account the non-official flows, this figure increases by approximately 50 per cent, and as much more again if we include the seasonal labour flows (see table 6).

On the trade front, cross-trade flows have increased more than four times in less than a decade (see chapter 3). The share of the European Union in the CEEC exports thus increased from less than 40 per cent to nearly 70 per cent today, which is equivalent to the

9. Deutsches Institut für Wirtschaftsforschung (German institute for economic research), Wochenbericht 21/2000, May 25, 2000).

exports of the member States to each other. Expressed as a percentage of the GDP of these economies, exports to the EU15 henceforth represent more than a third.

More important probably for the medium term is the productive integration by foreign direct investment (FDI) of European firms. The latter have expanded their economic area of operations in Europe by systematically including the candidate countries in their productive investments once the business environment became conducive and, above all, privatisation was introduced right away. These FDIs, of which more than two-thirds are from the EU, represents a quarter or more of productive investments in the candidate countries. Their orientation has played a greater role than their volume. A study by the European Commission has shown that less than a fifth of FDI received by the CEEC were used for delocalised industries or outsourcing, with the express aim of re-exporting the goods produced to the country of origin, thus allaying the fears of West European countries. However, approximately half of them are understood to have been directed towards the service industry, activities completely undeveloped during the communist period but that are essential to a modern economy, such as banks, community facilities and telecommunications. The rest of the FDI was used for local production to meet the current as well as the projected demand over the next ten years. All this boded well for the success of transition. For, as is obvious, direct capital flows can be critical for a healthy balance of payments position, which is chronically in deficit. But much more than that, it is the influx of new technologies and management methods that tilts the balance. All said and done these flows are the guarantee of a rise in productivity in the countries in transition to the West European levels, i.e. the convergence of the standard of living in the medium to long term.

On the other hand, the impact on the West European economies has been somewhat limited during the first phase, but it should not be under-estimated. In terms of growth, the mechanical contribution was no doubt marginal because of the very small aggregate GDP of the region and its initial shrinking : barely 2 per cent of the GDP of EU15 at the nominal exchange rate at the trough of the recession, in 1992-1993. Similarly, the flow of capital towards these economies hardly weighed on West Europe : the FDI by European enterprises to the CEEC did not represent more than 1 per cent of the total European investment. In comparison the cost of the German reunification for West Germany was at least 4 per cent per annum and its impact was felt by the whole of Europe because of the rise in interest rates. In terms of migration, according to official sources, the labour originating from these countries constitutes not more than 0.2 per cent of West European employment, and at worst can be double if casual or sporadic migration is included. This influx could hardly have weighed on the unemployment rate of the EU (8 per cent), nor on the average salaries, with the exception perhaps of certain categories of semi-skilled workers. In return, it made it possible to bring some relief to the habitual shortages (seasonal agricultural and construction labour in particular), including in Spain and Portugal. More significant on the other hand, trade between the two blocs is undeniably beginning to carry weight in the European Union. Exports to CEEC countries in fact grew from 4 per cent to nearly 12.5 per cent of exports to the rest of the world, and as much as 16 per cent to the Balkan countries, ranking just behind the United States. This trend can only reduce the impact of the global economic disruptions on Greater Europe.

But the real gains lie elsewhere : firstly, the EU found itself forced to elaborate/intensify and speed up its political and economic unification ; all the member States gradually realised that they had to prepare themselves for the entry of the new partners. A stronger Europe is clearly one of the pre-requisites for the success of enlargement. The successful entry of Greece into the Euro zone ; the perceptible change in the attitude of the United Kingdom in relation to a single currency ; the resonant debates on better governance in Europe ; the speedy implementation of the European directives, especially in relation to the single market, are probably some of the by-products of the prospect of enlargement that reinforce the economic solidity of the EU. For, if we ask the candidate countries to adopt the central points of the *acquis communautaire*, the famous 31 chapters of the current negotiation process, how can the 'old' members not comply with this *acquis* ! Similarly, the advantages of a single currency are even less questionable with 27 members than with 12. But on the other hand, the task of a real European economic policy is a complicated one and requires substantial progress on the part of European institutions, as two influential authors on the issue have stressed.[10]

Second indirect advantage : prosperity is within reach of the transition countries that have seriously initiated institutional economic reforms and have chosen the path of democratic stability. This especially refers to the Western Balkan region that followed a different path from the candidate countries. This region, which probably had a ten year lead over the satellite countries of the USSR, can measure the cost of its past mistakes against the fall in the standard of living and the complete about turn of the initial progress. We can at least hope that this painful period will help in the complete re-unification of the continent.

Ensuring that the Central and East European Countries Catch-up: Convergence

What we call catching-up or convergence is the economic process that enables an economically backward country or a group of countries to attain the level of another group of more advanced countries through a variety of push-pull effect mechanisms of the strong towards the weak.[11] The classic indicator is the level of per capita GDP expressed in terms of a comparable currency and above all in terms of the intrinsic comparable value of prices (one loaf of bread is equal to one loaf of bread...). What economists call parity of exchange rates and purchasing power (PPP), or standard of purchasing power (SPP), when calculated in relation to the average prices prevailing in the European Union. We now define the ratio between the average per capita GDP of the EU and that of the backward countries, and follow the trajectory of this indicator in the long duration. There is convergence when the ratio of the per capita GDP approaches unity. We can illustrate this by seeing how the catching-up process within the European Union fared between the years 1970-2000 and the evolution observed during the period 1960-1990 in two groups of countries : the East European countries and the South European countries that joined the EU in the eighties.

---

10. Pascal Lamy and Jean Pisani-Ferry, L'Europe de nos volontés, Plon, Paris, 2002.
11. The most obvious are the outlets provided by markets, such as the German market, for economies actually a hundred times smaller, like those of Hungary or the Czech Republic.

Firstly, we can clearly see the part played by the catching-up process within the European Union : the more backward a country, the quicker its rate of growth. Secondly, we can highlight the difference in evolution between countries that joined Europe in the eighties and that are now converging towards the European average, and the Eastern bloc countries, at the time members of Comecon, that in fact veered off, especially in the course of this same decade, regarded as the crisis point for the communist system.

The general trend of convergence within the EU is an almost unique case in economic history, apart from East Asia.[12]

To take the example of the four countries that joined the EU in the years between 1973 and 1985, convergence moved along four very different trajectories. Ireland is the symbol par excellence of the success of the theory of convergence. After many years of relative stagnation, the Irish economy came into its own in the mid-eighties, not only did it achieve the European average in 1966 but largely overtook it by the start of the new millennium. Spain and Portugal also made great strides, but more slowly, and their per capita GDP in 2002 remained below 80 per cent of the European average. For a long time Greece presented the counter-example of a successful convergence, for its per capita income remained stagnant and even decreased in relative terms, since the fall of the colonels' regime in 1974. It is only very recently, since its entry into the Euro zone in 2000, that an acceleration of the momentum of recovery has been observed. What is the effect of this catching-up on the Central and East European countries ?

The first method used by economists lay in adopting the theoretical approach developed by Robert J. Barro, in which variables such as human capital (educational level especially) play a key role. To this are added variables specific to the transition countries, especially the expected improvement in their institutional environment. The annual growth actually achieved fluctuates between +4 and +5 per cent, which clearly indicates these economies have come closer to the European average, the per capita growth potential of which is estimated currently to be 2 to 2.5 per cent at best. The second more classic method was tested by the European Commission

12. See Paul Krugman, Geography and Trade, Presses de l'Université de Louvain, Louvain.

and the Wifo.[13] It puts into play the effects of integration with a large unified market on the backward countries. The study conducted by the European Commission[14] principally highlights the double bonus that enlargement can constitute.

Simulations for the ten candidate countries show that their entry in the EU from 2005 will push their growth up from 3 per cent in a normal regime to 4 per cent in the central scenario and to 4.8 per cent in the optimistic scenario. The accrued gains in the decade 2000-2010 are likely to go up an additional 10 to 18 points of the GDP, according to the selected scenario. The optimistic scenario is however only possible if capital flows, and especially FDI and transfers (EU grants), are sufficient to finance the balance of payments structurally in deficit around 7 per cent of the GDP. The advantage of the optimistic scenario is that it shows that by generating a more rapid improvement in the standards of living, it reduces a corresponding need for financial assistance in the form of structural funds (regional aid) or a common agricultural policy.

For the EU15, the macroeconomic gains are obviously much smaller, as the CEEC represent merely 4 to 5 per cent of its GDP at current value. Accumulating over the entire decade, these gains do not exceed 0.5 to 0.7 additional points of the GDP, i.e. barely 0.1 per cent per annum for an expected annual growth of 2-2.5 per cent. But in return the costs of enlargement are also quite low. If they have not been assessed with great precision by the Commission in its 2001 study because the negotiations were still not complete, the Wifo study[15] puts their value at 190 billion Euros for the decade or 0.15 per cent of the GDP of EU15, that is merely a fraction of the global gains from growth.

The most interesting aspect of these studies lies in the estimation of the three major economic effects in play : gains from trade, gains from a more effective allocation of resources thanks to the single larger (economies of scale) and more competitive market, and lastly gains from migration. Paradoxically, the initial trade gains for the EU

13. Osterreichisches Institut für Wirtschaftsforschung (Austrian institute of econoomic research).

14. Enlargement paper, no. 4.

15. Fritiz Breuss, 'Macroeconomic Effects of EU Enlargement for Old and New Members', Wifo working paper, 143/2001.

are less significant as a result of trade liberalisation successfully implemented in the nineties, and because the commercial weight of these countries in the EU is still marginal : 1.3 per cent of the German GDP and 0.4 per cent of the French. On the other hand, the gains for the CEEC (close to one third) from access to a larger market in the very middle of the recovery phase are considerable. The common market effect represents half the growth benefits for the EU and as much for the CEEC, thanks to the transmission of the productivity gains to the entire zone and a correlative fall in price levels in the enlarged EU. The migratory effect eventually represents half the net gains for the EU in view of the contribution of a relatively skilled working population in a rapidly ageing zone. Inversely, it plays a slightly negative role for the CEEC because of the shortage of labour skilled in some countries, but after a not insignificant unemployment phase, resulting from transition, in the more populated countries such as Poland and Romania (see chap. 5).

The 2000-2002 Growth Cycle Substantiates the Process of Convergence and its Challenges

In 2000, the growth rate in real terms (outside inflation) of the 12 candidate countries was around +4.4 per cent as against +3.3 per cent in the EU15. In the course of this exceptional year for the global economy (the peak of the internet bubble), this difference of 1.1 point illustrates rather well the positive sum game set in motion by the enlargement process, but also its limits. In fact, to make good half the initial gap in the per capita GDP, a growth difference of 2 per cent over 35 years is necessary – the pace at which the EU countries converged among themselves from 1980 to 2000. The period is reduced to 23 years if it is 3 per cent. In 2001, however, the year of the reversal of the global scenario, the gap widened in favour of the CEEC countries, whose average growth went up to 3.1 per cent as against 1.5 per cent for the EU15. The gap even came close to 2 points in 2002 thanks to the greater resistance by the region, despite the fact that the more advanced countries started following the West European business cycle quite closely. In fact, the latter continued to benefit from three favourable factors : substantial FDIs, whose level continues to remain higher than elsewhere; a lesser reversal of exports, demonstrating the competitiveness of the newly installed capacities; and lastly, the impetus given by domestic consumption thanks to policies stimulating domestic demand in countries that were in a position to do this. Only Poland was not able to follow because of high but unbalanced growth during the boom period, but mainly because of a major conflict over economic policy between the Central Bank and the Finance Ministry, involved in a budgetary slide. Convergence from this point of view is only indicative of the potential to catch up, which does not mean certainty. Much depends on the quality of economic policies.

The Masses and Very Diverse Standards of Living

A global understanding of the region is helpful in determining the issues at stake in this new Europe. Nonetheless it conceals a triple factor of differentiation between the 12 candidate countries : the size of the market; the standard of living; and the convergence potential in relation to the European average. In terms of the real size of the market measured by the GDP in relation to the Standard of Purchasing Power (SPP), the major phenomenon is Poland's preponderant weight (more than a third of the GDP of the 12 applicants). Hence the feeling that a limited enlargement without the inclusion of Poland, as could have happened if the negotiations had hit a road block, would not really have made any economic sense. There remains, nevertheless, two-thirds of the region's GDP, in particular the second circle formed by Romania, which comes in second place along with the Czech Republic, which itself is slightly ahead of Hungary. The third circle is formed by small economies, very similar to each other, and each weighing about 5 per cent of the GDP of the applicant countries : Slovakia, the three Baltic states, and Bulgaria. The last circle is formed by the more developed countries but at the same time smaller with regard to the GDP : Slovenia, Cyprus and Malta.

In terms of the standard of living, expressed as a percentage of GDP, a major phenomenon is the even graduation of the 12 countries, ranging from the highest and quite close to the EU15 level (Cyprus), to the lowest four times below the said level (Bulgaria). During the period 1996-2000 alone this differentiation in the standard of living was coupled with differentiation in the pace of convergence of the various standards of living to the EU15 level.

Table 1.4

Growth, GDP and Forcast of Convergence Between the EU15 and the 12 New Member States

	Real GDP Growth			Total GDP Bn Current Euro		Total GDP Bn Euro SPP*			GDP per capita (SPA €)		GDP/capita and forcast (UE15=100)				
	Per cent				Per cent		Per cent	Per cent							
	2000	2001	2002p	2000	UE27	2000	UE27	PC12	1996	2000	1996	2000	2005	2010	2015
Bulgaria	5.8	.5	3.5	13.0	0.1	44.3	0.5	5	4600	5400	25	24	*27*	*30*	*33*
Czech R.	3.1	3.5	3.3	53.7	0.6	135.1	1.4	15	12000	13200	65	59	*64*	*71*	*78*
Estonia	6.4	5.4	4.0	5.4	0.1	12.1	0.1	1	6100	8400	33	37	*46*	*51*	*56*
Hungary	5.2	3.8	3.6	49.5	0.6	117.0	1.2	13	8600	11700	46	52	*59*	*65*	*72*
Latvia	6.6	7.6	5.0	7.7	0.1	15.6	0.2	2	4700	6600	25	29	*33*	*36*	*40*
Lithuania	3.3	5.3	3.5	12.2	0.1	24.3	0.3	3	5300	6600	29	29	*33*	*36*	*40*
Poland	4.0	1.1	1.5	171.0	1.9	337.9	3.6	36	6600	8700	36	39	*45*	*49*	*54*
Romania	1.6	5.3	4.0	40.0	0.4	135.4	1.4	15	6100	6000	33	27	*29*	*32*	*35*
Slovakia	2.2	3.3	3.5	9.5	0.1	58.3	0.6	6	8500	10800	46	48	*54*	*59*	*65*
Slovenia	4.6	3.0	3.0	20.9	0.2	32.0	0.3	3	12200	16100	66	72	*81*	*90*	*99*
Cyprus	4.8	4.5	4.5	19.5	0.2	12.4	0.1	1	14700	18500	79	82			
Malta	4.7	4.2	4.2	3.9	0.0	4.6	0.0	0	9400	11900	51	53			
CEECs 12	**4.4**	**4.3**	**3.6**	**406.3**	**4.6**	**929.0**	**10.0**	**100**	**6768**	**8139**	**38.9**	**39.2**			
EU15	3.3	1.5	1.0	8510.2	95.0	8510.2	90.0		18500	22500	100	100	*100*	*100*	*100*

Sources: Eurostat and WIIW, march 2002, for the forcasts

* SPP for Standart of Purchasing Power, the Eurostat computation of the real value of relative prices with the average EU=100

Apart from the special case of Cyprus and Malta, which are not transition economies, the winners are led by Slovenia, whose rate of development is twice the candidate countries' average and has progressed by 6 points in four years in relation to the EU15 level. Hungary gained 6 points and quickly closed in on the Czech Republic, which manifestly missed the first transition boat because of the 1997 crisis : it lost 6 points whereas Slovakia gained 2. Estonia also confirmed its reputation for dynamism with 4 additional points, which brought it close to the Polish level (and in fact overtook it in 2001).

The losers are situated along the Black Sea axis, with a loss of 6 points for Romania *vis-à-vis* the EU15 average for the same period. Bulgaria lost only one point but came in last among the candidate countries : 24 per cent of the average GDP of the EU15 countries. This situation proves the obvious correlation between distance from the centre of Europe and the degree of progress. It poses a real challenge : to enlarge in favour of the best students in the class and, at the same time, prevent the new peripheries from being caught up in a vicious circle. This problem has also prompted some experts to suggest an enlargement in the form of a 'big-bang', that is to say embracing the 12 applicant countries together, so as to stimulate a domino effect among the 12 backward countries, instead of incurring the risk of peripheralisation. The Laeken European Council (December 2001) finally decided upon a slightly different approach by conceiving enlargement in two phases, but with a much more voluntaristic programme for the two remaining countries : Romania and Bulgaria.

In terms of speed of convergence, the 1996-2000 assessment report was appended with the latest projections from the Austrian Institute WIIW[16] for the year 2015 (probably too pessimistic for the Baltic states). Most of the countries are *de facto* not dynamic enough to quickly cross the famous threshold of 75 per cent of the average per capita GDP of the EU, which officially separates the regions that are late in terms of development in comparison with the others. Only Slovenia, which has nearly crossed this threshold today, can overtake

16. Weiner Institut für Internationale Wirtschaft: Viennese institute for international economic studies. An independent organisation whose principal objective is the study of the transition economies of East Europe.

the European average (EU15 exclusively) by 2015. For all that, at the end of this decade, even the Czech Republic will be a few points short, while Hungary will probably cross the mark a little after 2015. Obviously it is for the most backward countries that the gap will still be very wide in 2015 : Bulgaria will just about have achieved one-third of the EU15 level, and Romania will not be too far ahead. These facts simply confirm that even with the powerful support of a bloc as important as the EU, catching-up is a very long drawn out exercise. More than just the formal accession to the EU in 2004 or 2007, the success of convergence of the candidate countries thus rests on the force of the dynamism put in motion by enlargement. The process of negotiations has often been maligned, especially its bureaucratic aspects and slowness. In reality, it has probably created sound conditions for the process of convergence for the next two to three decades. The example of South Europe corroborates that it is a reliable time frame, as the three countries concerned (Greece, Spain and Portugal) joined the Union between 1981 and 1986.

Benefits to the EU15 Group Should not be Under-estimated

Like any economic process, the enlargement of the European Union to incorporate the present 12 candidate countries includes costs and advantages that result in defensive and offensive positions. Therefore, not only do the net gains of such a process need to be spelt out but also the distribution of these costs and benefits among countries, among territories and among the different economic actors. Thus, often, the asymmetry of the gains in favour mainly of the CEEC, was probably responsible for some experts suggesting that extending enlargement to the East should be slowed down as the economic gains to the EU would barely represent 0.1 point of additional growth per annum. Why should one hurry and take risks to achieve EU cohesion when the economic benefits are so poor? Four arguments put things into perspective.

In the first place, seen from the angle of the greater EU27 and the global balance of power, the combined additional growth of the new Europe represents nearly 2 points of the GDP accruing over a ten-year period. In other words, a complete year's growth of the EU15;

this is not at all insignificant, if only in terms of employment. In terms of level, the gains realised by the full EU27 facilitate the stabilisation of Europe's relative share in the global economy, which has been steadily decreasing since the mid-70s.[17] In 2001, EU27 as a whole represented, according to the latest IMF figures, 22 per cent of the global GDP in terms of purchasing power parity, against 19.8 per cent for EU15 taken alone. This may seem low, but in reality only in 1987 did the EU have this type of influence in the world. Above all, EU27 is ahead of USA (21.3 per cent of the global GDP) and is thus the foremost group in the global economy.

True, the ongoing enlargement does not reverse the downward trend in the global economic weight of Europe, but it has slowed it down considerably. It is probably no mean task in the present context, for globalisation reinforces the role of the economic power in ensuring maximum room to manoeuvre, including when making certain crucial developmental choices. A good example is the implementation of the Kyoto protocol on climatic change, which pitted the two sides of the Atlantic against each other.

The second argument affirms that the longer we delay setting in motion the process of European enlargement, in particular by stabilising the environment of the transition countries in the medium term, the more we delay the real economic gains, i.e. a swifter convergence of these countries around the EU15 level, due to the effects of integration but also of accession at a more political level. Their potential GDP per capita being approximately three times higher than the actual level (28 per cent of the EU15 population as against 10 per cent of the GDP at comparable prices), it is after a 20 to 30 year time span that we can best measure the full impact of enlargement.

At this future date, the GDP of greater Europe will very probably increase by 15 to 20 points with just the 12 present candidate countries. And, through this, we can expect to secure the positive effects of a bigger market, i.e. nearly 500 to 600 million inhabitants strong. In other words much larger than that of the United States,

---

17. Expressed in terms of parity of purchasing power, the best measure no doubt for understanding the rise of developing countries, where, at the same time, domestic prices are always lower than prices in the rich countries.

probably even larger than China's, around the years 2030-2050, if we reason in terms of international purchasing power or solvent demand

The third argument states that the territorial asymmetry of the expected benefits to EU15 and the 12 applicants likely to gain maximum tangible benefits from enlargement, must be seen from a macroeconomic perspective, taking into account the impact on European firms. The latter are, in fact, the principal actors in the new markets, comprising 100 to 200 million additional people (including Turkey), where their investments amount to more than 75 per cent. Hence, the rapid recovery of these economies creates expectations of solid benefits at the level of global competitiveness. The much larger EU market results in economies of scale, as 80 per cent of FDI is destined for the domestic demand for goods and services. There are also gains from competition as a result of new locations, thus taking advantage of the competitive edge offered by these countries. The phenomenon is not limited to the shifting of factories from the West to the East. There are countless examples in the recent past of re-location of activities transferred and/or outsourced_to developing economies far away, particularly in Asia. As a result, besides the positive sectoral effects examined in Chapter 3, the macroeconomic loop becomes smaller, with fewer losses along the line between demand and supply, for 80 per cent of all that is spent comes back in the form of orders from Western Europe as against less than 10 per cent from Asia. If it is clear that the external structural deficit of the candidate countries contrasts with the structural surplus of Asia *vis-à-vis* Europe, it is just as clear that the financing of this deficit from West European savings reverts back in the form of demand for products and equipment to the present EU in very high proportion.

Finally, the argument that we must offset the low net benefits for EU15 against the other option, namely non-enlargement or a slowing down of the process. This opportunity cost[18] of non-enlargement is both political and economic. With regard to the economic aspect, let us remember that the expected growth for EU15 is divided equally between migratory benefits, which compensate for a rapidly ageing population, and efficiency gains on the model of the

18. This traditional economic concept can be simply defined as the cost of the choice of not using the most acceptable solution.

1993 single market. Must one give this up? On the political front, the region's specialists[19] have continued to warn us about the risk of stirring the old demons of Central Europe, a reminder of which is the Balkan war. Just as the implicit driving force of the 1957 Treaty of Rome was the Franco-German rapprochement, in the same way the ongoing enlargement is a political promise made on the morrow of the fall of the Berlin Wall in November 1989, to reunite the European continent around the principles of democracy and peace. All the opinion polls, such as those conducted by Eurobarometer, are unequivocal about this aspiration of the peoples of East and West Europe alike to reunite their continent.

In relation to the Member States, one of the latest opinion polls on the subject by Eurobarometer (June 2002) provide three major types of information on enlargement:

1) Europeans who feel that they are not well informed and not very involved : 83 per cent of the interviewed felt they were not well informed on enlargement as against barely 1 per cent very well informed and 12 per cent well informed. In these circumstances, it is not surprising to find that 1 per cent of the population considers itself deeply involved against 57 per cent not at all involved and 27 per cent slightly involved;
2) Europeans who nevertheless say that they are on the whole in favour in principle : 14 per cent only say they are against any type of enlargement as against 65 per cent in favour of accession, whether it is certain countries (44 per cent) or all the countries that so wish (21 per cent). 15 per cent only do not have an opinion;
3) Their motivations seem to be much more political than economic : only one out of ten interviewed feels that his life will be better after enlargement, mainly because of the advantages of a bigger market. Only a small percentage of the interviewees consider that it will deteriorate, especially because of the greater risk of unemployment. On the other hand, 64 per cent consider that the change of scale in the

19. In particular Jacques Rupnik, the author of L'autre Europe, Le Seuil, Paris, 1993 and, more recently, the viewpoint of the Czech President, Vaclav Havel.

EU will not have much impact on their lives, and that their motivation is predominantly political : the reunification of the European continent.

Distribution of the Costs-Benefits of Enlargement: A Sensitive Subject

The distribution of the costs-benefits of enlargement is by nature a sensitive topic. Firstly, of course, on the budgetary front, and this on two counts : who should pay and what. The asymmetry that emerges from the first budgetary and agricultural proposals made by the European Commission in the spring of 2002 opposes, for instance, the rich and the poor countries, on the one hand, and on the other, the major agro-food producers and the others. The richer and least agricultural countries say that they do not wish to pay 'twice', or otherwise they should be given guarantees regarding the effectiveness of the European policies in the fields of agriculture and regional development, which will absorb three-fourths of the allocated sums (10 to 15 billion Euros per annum from 2004 to 2006), and nearly double thereafter, or 0.25 per cent of the EU15 GDP). Thus, just like the reform of the European institutions, enlargement has become a complicated issue. Should the Common Agricultural Policy (CAP) be amended, and how? Should one continue with a cohesion policy in favour of the more underprivileged regions? Should the Union have its own Budget and should it be more than 1.27 per cent of the Union's GDP, a benchmark established at the Berlin European Council in March 1999? For the moment, the budgetary compromise made in Copenhagen only covers the three initial years of accession. The full debate will therefore take place over the new five-year budget 2007-2013, i.e. after the European elections of 2004, and in the presence of the new members.

On the macroeconomic front and from a purely economic point of view, i.e. cost-benefit calculations, some of the results available, like those of Wifo and the European Commission, clearly show a net advantage for the Union : +0.35 to +0.50 points for EU15. In terms of the individual Member States, the distribution is however quite unequal, with a group of 4 big gainers - Austria, Italy, Germany and Ireland (around +0.6 points of the cumulated GDP from 2005 to

2010), seven countries are approximately average, and there are four losers, including Spain and Portugal, with about -0.2 points. For France, the net benefit is positive (+0.15 points) but 2.5 less than the average benefit accruing to the EU and 4.5 times less than that of Germany. These results should be viewed with caution, but they provide a fairly accurate picture.

On the whole, if most of the work on the rationality of enlargement towards the East, concludes that the net result of enlargement appears to be positive on the economic front, Europe will nevertheless experience fresh upheavals because of it. The cost-benefit distribution management is coupled with major institutional changes, as is demonstrated by the striking parallel between the negotiations on enlargement, the work of the European Convention on the future of the Union, presided by the former President Valéry Giscard d'Estaing, and that, increasingly frequent, of economists and public figures who are questioning the regulatory capacity of the new Europe, which besides expanding horizontally has had to penetrate deeper in order to make enlargement possible. Everything definitely depends on the quality of the preparation of the institutions both in the West and in the East, and the effective control of the process to avoid a budgetary, social or economic slide. This was the objective of the enlargement negotiations initiated in Copenhagen in June 1993. Nine years later, the second Copenhagen European Council constitutes one of the first positive conclusions. As we can see enlargement is a long process.

2

The Virtuous Logic of Integration: FDI and Consumption Catching-up

The success of transition in central Europe is less due to the orthodox economic policies or the exclusive priority given to institutional reforms than to the combined action of a decisive virtuous cycle between the effects of supply and demand. This has served as the fulcrum for the two first constituents (successful economic stabilisation policies and market reforms) and made their success possible.[20] Here we encounter the lessons learnt from a comparison of the difficulties of the Russian transition and the most positive results of the Chinese transition.[21] In the case of the CEEC, the proximity of a powerful Europe encouraged West European manufacturers to undertake strategic direct investment operations (FDI) right from the initial months of transition, starting with the nearest countries. In view of their mass effect, these transfers of know-how greatly contributed to stabilising the free falling economies after the 1989 shock. But what is probably more important is that they contributed in disseminating the EU institutional norms whose positive impact could be measured in real time by peoples and governments.

European companies did not enter the CEEC primarily because of the low salaries and the possibility of delocalisation/outsourcing, unlike FDI in many emerging countries, and especially in Asia in the seventies. This process only concerns 20 per cent of the operations undertaken in the first decade of transition. It is above all the lure of the additional demand constituted by 100 million people, and

20. Richard E. Baldwin, *Towards an Integrated Europe*, CEPR (Center for Economic Policy Resarch), London, 1994.

21. Despite highly controversial, we can find a good analysis of these differences in Joseph Stiglitz, Globalization and its Discontents, W. W. Norton & Company, New York, 2002.

more than that the possibility of demand catching-up with West European standards that has caught the attention of the major international groups, primarily West European, but also of a great number of neighbouring small and medium enterprises. The idea is to capture as quickly as possible a large market share in these new centres of demand. The cutthroat competition in which the two automobile giants Volvo and Renault have been engaged for the takeover of the largest automobile constructor in the region, Skoda, is a good example. Another illustration on the grand scale of the virtuous demand-supply combination is the entry of modern large-scale distribution, which has invested billions of Euros in the area since 1992-93, and penetrated the most backward provinces and countries in its unrelenting race to capture the market share. The opening of the first Carrefour department store in Romania in early 2002 is a good example. All the economic authorities of Central Europe acknowledge its powerful impact on disinflation. The same is true of the modernisation of the logistical and supply channels, something which was probably just as important as all that had been achieved in the financial sectors, although rather belatedly. Lastly, the rapid modernisation of distribution is at the very heart of the process of convergence of the consumption structures and patterns between the two Europe, for it guarantees a deep-rooted unification of the continent.

A Region that is Becoming Important for FDI Flows Towards Emerging Countries

With a flow of 1270 billion dollars as against 1080 billion in 1999, global FDI has, according to UNCTAD, set a new record in 2000. With 23 billion dollars of incoming flows, i.e. 1.8 per cent of the total, the 12 candidate countries in the EU cut a sorry figure. In reality the enormous FDI flows among developed countries have to be excluded with that year in particular a record number of mergers-acquisitions registered. Instead the Central and East European countries have to be compared with the group of developing countries alone. Insignificant at the beginning of the decade, the weight of the CEEC zone *vis-à-vis* the developing countries (excepting China and Hong Kong) in reality has continued to increase : from 7.7 per cent on an average in 1988-93, their share grew to 17 per cent in 2000. Moreover, the 10 per cent increase in the FDI to Eastern Europe in 2000, contrasted with the general decline towards developing countries. With a population of barely a hundred million people, the 12 CEEC countries attract more than half the total FDIs to China, or approximately an equivalent amount, if we exclude the intra-Chinese capital flows with Taiwan and Hong Kong, 50 per cent of which are for the purpose of fiscal benefits.[22]

This attraction of the CEEC has continued to strengthen with the prospect of accession. While UNCTAD noted a fall of 40 per cent to 50 per cent of FDI in the world for the years 2001 and 2002, which were marked by a reversal of the global situation, the flow of FDI to the CEEC have continued to progress slightly. For UNCTAD, this difference with the other regions is due to two factors : a constant and steady increase of the attractiveness rating because of an improvement in the business environment ; and proximity in the context of an anticipated accession to the EU in the near future.

The Increasing Global Attractiveness of the CEECs

The global attractiveness of the CEECs can be measured by the new indicator which was introduced in the 2001 UNCTAD report[23] on direct investments : FDI index or the IIFDI incomings.[24] The rise of the 10 Central and East European countries as a newly emerging zone can be seen from the evolution of this index. The latter, close to 0 between 1988-90, exceeded 1.2 average in 1998-2000, or 20 per cent more than its global economic weight. At the same time, the index of the developing countries as a whole only progressed marginally (0.6 to 0.7) and the Chinese index progressed from 0.8 to 0.9. Some countries such as Turkey and Malaysia even suffered a setback, from 0.5 to 0.1 and from 2.6 to 1 respectively. The index of the Mediterranean countries (North Africa, Israel and Egypt) remained stable around 0.6. This does not mean that the CEEC has emerged by taking the place of the Mediterranean countries, even if

22. Boïllot J.J., "The New Economic Geography of Asia," *China Perspectives No.30*, July - August 2000, pp. 18-25, www.cefc.com.hk/
23. UNCTAD, *World Investment Report*, UNCTAD, Geneva (yearly report)
24. IIFDI or Index of Incoming FDI: this rating compares a country's share in the global FDI in relation to the global weight of its GDP, its working population and its exports; it is 1 if the two are equal, and correspondingly more if the country receives more FDI than its normal weight in the global economy.

the ratio of 2:1 between the two zones indicates a basic difference in their integration potential with the European space. This is even truer of Turkey. Among the CEEC, four groups can be distinguished:

1) Two economies, Hungary and Slovenia, currently converging towards the foreign investment levels of Spain and Portugal with an IIFDI index of 1.6 and 0.8 respectively.[25] For these two Central European countries it is important to know whether they will remain as they are or follow in the footsteps of the small highly specialised European economies, like those of Finland (3.7) and Sweden (8.5), which continue to attract FDI thanks to the constant improvement of their competitive edge.

2) Two very promising economies because of their dynamism, the Czech Republic and Estonia, which in the last period have received twice as much FDI as their weight in the world (IIFDI = 2). In comparison, Spain and Portugal in 1988-90, just after their accession to the EU, had an index of 4.2 and 2.9 respectively. Malta, which is catching-up very fast, has an index of 5. We can deduce from this that the flow of FDI to the most promising CEE countries will probably continue to increase significantly in the coming years.

3) A group constituted by Poland, Bulgaria, Latvia and Lithuania has a regional average of 1.2. In other words, the IIFDI of these countries is above their global economic weight, but still very much below the levels noted at the time of accession of the South European countries in 1986. In this context we can talk of countries with a high potential in the short term, if the conditions for economic liberalisation in these economies continue to improve.

4) The last group of countries below their expected potential (IIFDI = 1) follow two types of trajectories : the take-off phase, like Slovakia (IIFDI = 1), or below their catching-up potential like Romania (0.8). However, the force of the European integration movement can be gauged just by this last figure. The most mediocre index is still superior to the

25. It should be specified that the FDI statistics for Slovenia are a little under-valued as they do not take into account domestic reinvestments. However, this should not change the order of magnitude of the given figures.

Mexican index (0.7) and equal to the Chinese index in 1988-1990, i.e. at the height of the liberalisation phase of the Chinese economy. To counterbalance this optimistic vision, the Greek index is very low (0.3). The same is true of Cyprus, a country that ranks below Egypt. There is no way of ruling out scenarios of this type in central Europe if the transition process gets derailed or if the distance factor creates a new European periphery diverging from the dynamic core of the continent.

Table 2.1

FDI Performance Index 1998-2000

Malta	4,6	Irland	5,1	Hong Kong	5,9
Czech Rep*	2,5	Sweden	4,1	Argentina	1,4
Hungary	1,1	Netherland	3,3	Chile	2,3
Estonia	2,3	Denmark	2,8	Brazil	1,3
CEECs 10	**2,1**	UK	1,8	India	0,2
Poland	1,4	Finland	1,9	China	1,2
Bulgaria	1,8	Germany	1,3	Mexico	0,7
Latvia	1,6	France	0,8	**average DCs**	**0,7**
Lithuania	1,5	Spain	1,1	Tunisia	0,8
Slovakia	1,5	Austria	0,7	Korea	0,6
Romania	1,0	Portugal	0,9	Egypt	0,5
Slovenia	0,3	Italy	0,2	Morocco	0,4
Cyprus	0,4	Greece	0,1	Turkey	0,1

Source: World Investment Report 2002, UNCTAD Geneva (some figure may differ from the text which mention the 2001 report Index

* The UNCTAD index compare the share of one country in the world inward FDI with its share in the world GDP, in the global labor force and the worl export. It is greater than 1 when the country gets a ratio greater than the world average

What are the attractiveness factors of CEEC? Among all the studies conducted on the principal determinants of the FDI level, four factors often reappear, which combine the neo-classical approach in terms of the relative cost of factors and the New economic geography approach of which the best known exponent is the theoretician, Paul Krugman.[26] The four factors are : a demand effect linked to the size of the market, and especially the anticipated size, hence the importance of the imminent accession to the EU ; a human

26. Paul Krugman, *Geography and Trade*, Presses de l'Université de Louvain, 1991.

capital and its cost effect ; a quality of institutions effect that can be compared to the investors intention to minimize the market approach costs ; and lastly, the external geography effects, i.e. the attraction or isolation of the periphery in relation to the dynamic centres of the global economy.

Human Capital and its Cost: A Picture of Contrasts

As far as human capital is concerned, the wage level has clearly not been the discriminatory factor within the zone itself. The lowest salaries are found in countries, which hold the least promise for foreign investors, such as Bulgaria or Romania as opposed to Hungary or the Czech Republic. But it is true that it is not so much the level of salaries that counts than, what we call the unit cost of wages, i.e. the total wage cost in relation to the market value of production. However, the data available shows that the correlation is also quite weak even if we take productivity into account. Hungary and Romania thus top the list of countries with the lowest unit cost of wages, but their per capita FDI or as a proportion of GDP is in the ratio of 1:5 (see figure 2.1).

Figure 2.1

Index of Unit Labour Cost (UE15=100) in 1999

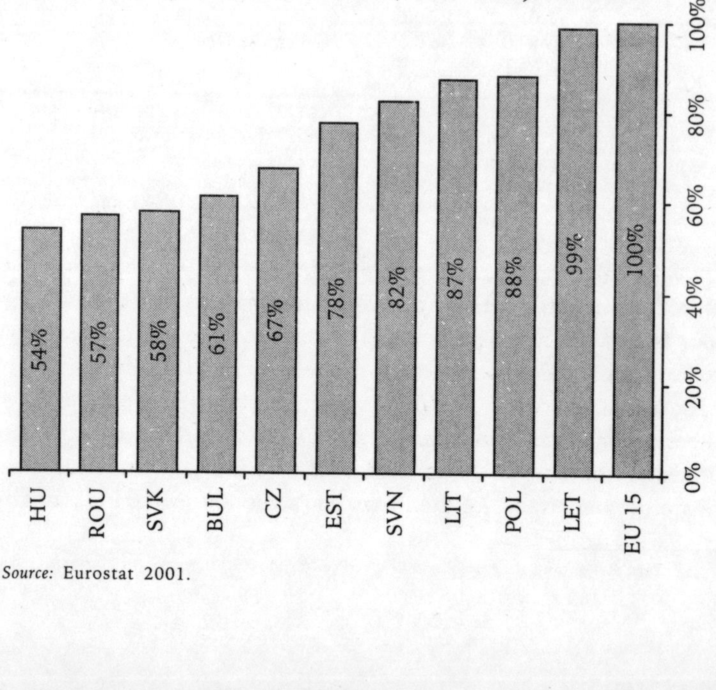

Source: Eurostat 2001.

The reason for this weak correlation to salaries is connected to the investors' motivations, which have been highlighted in a study by the EU services.[27] Nearly 50 per cent of FDI has been directed towards the non-exchangeable domestic sectors, for example services like telecommunications, water, banks, etc. With regard to the other 50 per cent, more vulnerable to international competition, 30 per cent of FDI has been directed at markets considered promising and where there are none or few Western firms present, for the purpose of manufacturing locally, as soon as conditions, i.e. costs, justify it. Only 20 per cent of FDI are directed at relatively labour intensive sectors, whose end objective is to export.

On the other hand, all the studies available show that the level of human capital is an important determinant for investors in the CEEC, whatever the orientation sought. What is the level in this region? The skill level of workers in the East European countries has resulted in specific measures being taken by Eurostat, especially in a pan-European comparative perspective. The overall picture presents some interesting contrasts.

The widespread belief that the candidate countries have a good level of education is a misleading one. It is true at the primary school level, for 100 per cent literacy has been achieved in most countries. Similarly, only 18 per cent in the 25-29 age group have a low educational level, which is paradoxically half the EU percentage. But where higher education of the working population is concerned, which is a determining factor for the economy, it is clearly below the EU average : 15 per cent and 21 per cent respectively.

What is the difference due to? A real hypertrophy of middle level education - it applies to more than two thirds of the workers in the CEEC, against 43 per cent in the EU15. This is partly due to a statistical illusion. The communist regimes included in the middle educational level, the short continuing education programmes, but whose content was rather poor. These were intended for students who had left the educational system prematurely. It is also, broadly speaking, the result of a hypertrophy on the part of industry : 47 per cent of the average GDP of these countries in 1990, against 33 per cent today and less than 25 per cent in the EU15. The undeniable

27. European Commission, DG ECFIN, *The Economic Impact of Enlargement*, 2001.

image of a qualified industrial labour is offset by a certain anachronism in the general levels of education and the new technological and organisational paradigms of industry. This deficiency clearly emerges from the opinions expressed by Western investors present in the CEEC.

Seen from this angle, middle level education in the candidate countries is not really favourable for the rapid economic recovery of the new members.[28] However, it is only an average we are talking about here. The data has to be modulated because of the considerable difference between countries, especially in view of the regional basin effects, which is reminiscent of the North/South axis in the EU15 :

Baltic side : Estonia is in second position in the 27-strong Europe Union, alongside Finland and not far from all the Nordic countries that have more than 30 per cent workers having attained higher studies. Latvia, especially because of its young Russian workers with higher education and Lithuania (24 per cent workers with higher education, as in Germany) fall in this group;

Central Europe basin, more heterogeneous, has a profile somewhat similar to that of Germany and Austria, i.e. with greater emphasis on secondary education than on high-tech. Leaving the others behind, Slovenia and Hungary are at the top but below Greece as far as higher education is concerned (15 per cent of the working population). Poland and the Czech Republic have record middle level education (> 70 per cent), which corresponds well with the image one has of *Man of Iron*,[29] a Wajda film. An image that Slovakia shares but with a higher education level that is even lower (9 per cent);

The extreme Eastern part of the Balkans is also quite heterogeneous with Bulgaria in a better position than Romania, for example. But the predominance of the middle level education and the large-scale migration of graduates from Bulgaria does not make it easy to distinguish it from Romania with regard to the percentage of workers with higher education, which barely exceeds 10 per cent.

28. The EU average, already inadequate, comes down by two points in the higher education sphere when we shift from 15 to 27 countries.

29. In other words a robust, courageous labourer, clever too but with a low educational level.

The effectiveness of the educational policies is therefore crucial for the future Member States. The present audit does not pose much of a problem from this point of view. The average public expenditure on education, according to the World Bank, was around 5.4 per cent of the GDP in 1997, as against 5.6 per cent in the EU15. Ireland, which has been rather successful in catching-up, allocated more than 6 per cent of its GDP over two decades. Today, it has 23 per cent of its working population with higher education, i.e. as much as Germany.

The Importance of the Institutional Environment

The institutional environment and the implementation of reforms constitute essential criteria for investors in Central Europe. Transition indexes developed by EBRD in the early nineties can, in particular, act as indicators of the quality of reforms carried out. If we consider the synthetic index and take the sub-indexes according to the field of reforms, the statistics in the last annual report of the United Nations Commission for Europe, establish a definite correlation between the quality of institutional change and the level of FDI expressed as a percentage of GDP. The correlation ratio R2 was 0.88 in 1996 (the closer it is to 1, the greater the correlation), i.e. in the middle of the strategic investment phase in Eastern Europe.

Its decrease to 0.45 in the 2000 data does not imply that this factor no longer plays a prominent role among the post-communist transition countries, and especially among the CEEC and the former USSR. This weaker correlation on the other hand, impacts upon the Central European group. While the per capita FDI level of Poland, the Czech Republic and Hungary diverged considerably in 2000, since 1995, they have recorded the same level of the synthetic EBRD index with regard to the quality of institutions. This can be explained by the second wind that CEEC's attractiveness has earned it : once the critical threshold of market reforms has been crossed, other factors come into play, namely the quality of the adoption of the *acquis* or the competitiveness of the economies, which is the classic fare for Europeans. Probably what surprises the most in the initial phase is the strong correlation between the quality of the institutional environment and the proximity of the EU. As if the geographical factor was the most important explanatory variable, a fact which has been admitted by the best experts on the subject.[30] Why?

The Proximity of EU15: A Powerful Factor of Attraction

The countless historical examples reveal the considerable role that capital flows can play in promoting trade between an advanced country and a backward periphery, once the latter opens itself to international trade. This can be seen in the case of Japan and the Asian New Industrialised Countries (NICs) in the eighties (but with all the institutional limitations of the Japanese model) and between USA and Mexico in the mid- nineties. The magnitude of the pull action is due to an initial asymmetry : what constitutes small amounts for a developed region represents very important productive capital flows for the peripheral zone. This is coupled with institutional effects implicitly produced by work habits and foreign investment. This phenomenon seems to have fully worked between the EU and the CEEC and should continue in the coming years via the accession negotiations.

From the European perspective, the Central and East European countries (CEEC) only represent 3 per cent of the total FDI flows for the period 1994-99, and 6 per cent of the extra-EU flows. They have nevertheless received one-third of the European FDI towards emerging zones and henceforth represent more than 20 per cent of the assets held by the EU countries in these zones. From 0 in 1990, the annual flows are now close to 15 billion Euros, although they are concentrated in specific countries : an overall 75 per cent in the trio of Poland – Czech Republic – Hungary. With the accession of 12 countries in 2007, an extension of the phenomenon is very likely to take place between now and 2007. The evolution of the absolute amounts especially illustrates the reigning asymmetry between the two parts of Europe. The CEEC figure increasingly in the European Foreign Direct Investments (FDI), but remain marginal in relation to the total European FDIs, whether it is intra-EU or directed towards the rest of the world. Thus, the flows towards the United States alone in 1999 (180 billion Euros) amounted to four times the accrued total assets of the EU in the Central and East European countries.

---

30. Claudia M. Buch, Daniel Piazolo, 'Capital and Trade Flows in Europe and the Impact of Enlargement', Kiel Institute of World Economics, *Kiel Working Paper No. 1001*, September 2000.

Figure 2.2

EU15 Outward FDI flows (Bn €)

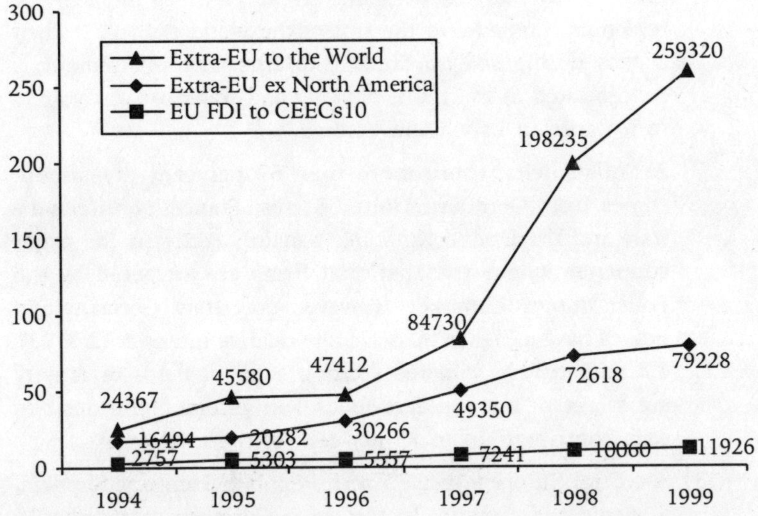

Source: Eurostat, European Union Foreign Direct Investment, Yearbook 2000.

Seen from the CEEC angle, on the other hand, the FDIs from Europe constitute nearly 70 per cent of their direct incoming investment, with a significant amount coming from cross-border countries (80 per cent if we include the maritime borders), which is a strong indication of the integrative neighbourly relations (see Fig. 2.2). The full measure of the market proximity effect can be seen from the manner of distribution of the European FDIs per investor-country, particularly by reverting to a relative intensity indicator of the FDIs (RII). The latter correlates the weight of a European investor in the CEEC with its average weight in the global FDIs. Thus it is 1 if the two weights coincide and all the more high if the two countries are closely integrated through investment. The geographic orientation of the investing countries that is revealed by this indicator highlights the net effects of the regional basins. Germany is thus the primary investor [in relation to the total FDI stock] in the region (20 per cent), but Austria has the most concentrated investments with a relative intensity (RII) 22 times greater than its weight in the world ! With the help of this indicator, four economic belts have been formed to date:

1) A Baltic sea belt of small countries : Sweden, Finland, Denmark represent approximately 55 per cent of incoming FDIs to the Baltic states, and invest 17 times more in the region as compared to the rest of the world (RII=17). Their access to the sea no doubt explains why investment is concentrated in the trade, banking and transport sectors and in logistics in Latvia and Estonia.

2) A Polish belt, where more than 67 per cent investment comes from Germany, United States, France, Netherlands, Italy and the United Kindom. It mainly concerns the major countries whose transnational firms are attracted by the Polish domestic market. However, only Italy, Germany and France have a higher than average relative intensity (2.6, 2.0, 1.8 respectively). On the sectoral side, all fields of activity are targeted, but the agro-foods and automobile industries each contribute up to 25 per cent of the total stock;

3) A central European belt : Czech Republic, Hungary, Slovakia, Slovenia and Croatia. In this zone Germany represents 24 per cent of FDI with an intensity of 2.7, but by itself Austria accounts for nearly 20 per cent and invests 50 times more than in the rest of the world. With relative intensities that are much weaker on the whole, United States and Netherlands each contribute approximately 13 per cent to this group. This is a manifestation of the strategy followed by international firms, of which the biggest are American and many are based in The Netherlands (or Switzerland). In the cenral European belt, the FDIs are mainly concentrated in the automobile sector (Czech Republic, Hungary, Slovakia, and Slovenia), chemicals (Hungary and Croatia, two-thirds of the FDIs in the region), agro-foods (strong in Hungary, weak in the Czech Republic and in Poland), and lastly electronics (Hungary). In other words, sectors that are increasingly becoming globalised. Unlike Poland, what is clearly noticeable in this zone is the extreme specialisation of the small economies.

4) A belt comprising the eastern Balkan states, ignored by investors until the end of the Yugoslavian war, but which is now catching up rapidly. Besides, the situation is influenced

by the fact that textiles-clothing and furniture do not require heavy direct investment, as sub-contracting and trading can be substituted (see chapter 4). We note, on the other hand, that the machinery and equipment sector attracted 1.4 billion Euros in Romania, which is in second position after neighbouring Hungary. In this zone the highest relative intensities are attributed to Italy and Austria, (neighbourhood effect), France (effect of going around the many borders separating it from the CEEC) and lastly, the United States (globalisation effect, as in the other countries).

Competitiveness of the CEEC and Competitiveness of Greater Europe

While the competitiveness of the emerging European economies is all too often measured in terms of wage costs or market size, the *Global Competitiveness Report 2001*[31] by the World Economic Forum proposes an interpretative grid and much more pertinent measures. Professors Jeffrey Sachs and Michael Porter specify that the competitiveness factors depend on the level of development of each country. The assessment of the level of competitiveness should favour a time scale perspective rather than a country scale basis for a given year. What is the use of increasing R&D (Research and Development) expenditure in low income countries, like Romania and Bulgaria, where the economy is driven by simple production factors and has greater need of modern infrastructure? In contrast, labour – skilled-semi-skilled does not help much in economies of the higher group, such as Slovenia or Hungary, whose competitiveness depends more on their capacity for technological assimilation. The international ranking established by the World Economic Forum should be interpreted in terms of the level of development of each group and not merely on the basis of the 1 to 75 scale, as many commentators do. With this prefatory detail in mind, the 2001 report offers two types of lessons on the CEEC zone and its potential for an extremely positive role in the promotion of European competitiveness on the global scale.

None of the candidate countries of course are well placed in comparison with the leading group of the technologically most

31. Part of the 2001 report of the World Economic Forum is available on the website www.weforum.org

competitive countries, where only the developed countries are present. On the other hand, the second group of 'economies driven by investment' starts off with the trio formed by Hungary (just behind Italy), Estonia and Slovenia. In the middle is the Czech Republic (on the same level as Greece) and a little further Slovakia, Poland (level of Mexico) and the two remaining Baltic countries. The CEEC group thus seems to be relatively well placed among the emerging countries. The advanced indicator of the evolution of competitiveness calculated by M. Porter nevertheless denotes a rather dull trend in the last few years. It is favourable for Hungary and Estonia, but neutral for Poland and Slovakia and even negative for the Czech Republic, whose relative progress has been rather slow in the last four years. Lastly, the third group called 'economies driven by the factors of production', shows Romania and Bulgaria rubbing shoulders with Turkey and Vietnam, without much indication either of any decisive progress in the relative scale of the group. It is a realist vision that is ultimately shared by many investors who have been interviewed. What is the reason, therefore, for so much FDI to find its way to central Europe, especially from the neighbouring European countries?

Economic geography in fact shows that there is a strong complementarity between the advanced European countries and the CEEC, each of which is part of one of the three geographic sub-zones indicated above. The integration of these countries because of the impetus given by their advanced European neighbours, exerts a domino effect over the whole and enables the reinforcement of European competitiveness at the global level. This could be defensive (protection of the European market) or offensive (increased competitiveness in other major zones of the world).[32] Exaggerating somewhat, one could say that the Nordic champions, such as Finland, and Sweden, help The Baltic countries and regions, like Estonia, but also, to a certain extent, Poland; in return their competitiveness draws upon the advantages of the CEEC. In the centre, the Germany-Austria group helps the remaining Polish regions, the Czech Republic, Slovakia, Hungary and Slovenia. In the South, Italy's strong points, in industries that need more labour from neighbouring areas, effectively serve in Romania, Bulgaria, and in former Yugoslavia.

32. A good example is the plan to export small Volkswagen cars manufactured in Slovakia to the United States.

These complementarity effects also intervene rather forcefully in the adoption of economic policies favourable to the dynamic competitivity of the candidate countries, such as educational investments or infrastructure. Concretely speaking, this is what happens when the Austrian or Italian transporters exert pressure on their neighbours to renovate their highways as quickly as possible. Or when the PSA (Peugeot Automobile) group negotiates with the Czech authorities to share the training expenses of workers in the automobile industry, who will thereafter be employed in its new Kolin factory (see chapter 4).

A FDI Potential which has not even Remotely been Achieved in the Early 2000s

The present concentration (up to 78 per cent) of FDI in three countries of the region (Poland, Hungary and Czech Republic) logically denotes a good margin of progress in the coming years. Indeed, the backward countries are gradually manifesting a desire to push reforms, especially because of the impact of the implementation of the *acquis communautaire*. However, the difference in the pace of catching-up with the first wave of countries, is also an incentive. A simple calculation based on the current country-wise levels of FDI, shows that only achieving a benchmark of 2000 dollars per capita should push the FDI stock in the region to approximately 200 billion dollars in the coming decade.

This order of magnitude is in keeping with the work done at the Kiel Institute on the attraction potential of the CEEC for the FDIs as a result of the gravitational effect around the European Union, coupled with the accession process. The model used seeks to explain quantitatively the direct investment flows of the EU15 with the help of six geographical-economic variables : per capital GDP, population, the monetary aggregate M2[33]/GDP ratio, the imports/GDP level, distance between countries, and lastly membership or non-membership of the EU. What are the results of this model?

Despite the explosion of FDI inflows towards the CEEC during the nineties decade, in 1998 these only constituted 47 per cent of the potential calculated by the Kiel Institute model. In view of their economic weight, their geographical location and their imminent

33. The aggregate M2 includes M1 (bank notes and coins, sight deposits) + term deposits and deposits at notice.

accession to the EU, nearly 75 billion dollars at the very least should make their way to these countries. Considering their relatively rapid growth in the last few years, the total stock could even reach 250 billion dollars by 2010, against a little more than 120 billion registered in 2001.

Within the CEEC, the Kiel Institute's study distinguishes three groups. Hungary is alone in the first group, and is already close to completing the theoretical stock of a Member State. This signifies that in the future, the evolution of the FDI flows to this country will depend primarily on the growth of domestic demand and the opening up of trade. A second group comprises Poland, the Czech Republic and Estonia, which countries only achieved 35 per cent to 50 per cent of their theoretical level in 1998. The third group includes four countries with a theoretical potential which is even greater : Romania, Lithuania, Bulgaria and Slovakia. It appears, moreover, that this catching-up potential is on its way to becoming a reality, if we are to believe the data for 2001 and 2002 and the announcement of such major projects as the buyout in Slovakia of the public gas producer operator, SPP, for a sum of 3.1 billion Euros.[34]

Table 2.2

Stock of FDI in CEECs

	Mds USD	*% CEECs*	*USD/Hab*
Bulgaria	3.9	3.0	465
Czech R.	26.8	21.0	2608
Estonia	3.2	2.5	2234
Hungary	23.6	18.5	2338
Latvia	2.2	1.7	928
Lithuania	2.7	2.1	724
Poland	42.4	33.4	1095
Romania	7.6	6.0	341
Slovakia	6.1	4.8	1135
Slovenia	3.3	2.6	1634
Cyprus	2.2	1.8	2861
Malta	3.3	2.6	8637
CEEC12	127.2	100.0	1203

Source: World Investment Report 2002, UNCTAD Geneva.

34. In 2002, GDF, Gazprom and Ruhrgas were retained as SPP's strategic partners with 49 per cent of the group's capital but with a voting majority.

It is interesting to note that another study by the same Institute[35] shows that this diversion of FDI towards the CEEC is not detrimental to the South European countries, at least when it involves investment flows from the German zone. In other words, the European Union enlargement towards the East constitutes a positive sum game and not a zero sum game, and this includes actually all the emerging European countries considered to be natural candidates for membership in the future. It is one of the major themes of reflection of the next few years on the respective evolution of the principal developing zones that surround the developed core of the European Union. Some analysts are concerned about the Mediterranean zone in particular. If it is true that the CEEC is offering competition in some industries (see textiles-clothing in chapter 4), there are many indications that the complementarity of comparative advantages is stronger and that this competition on the contrary is a stimulating factor for the backward countries. Indeed, the latter can ascertain the positive results of the successful integration within a pan-European economic space.

Table 2.3

FDI Potential of Progress with or without EU Membership

bn USD	*BUL*	*CR*	*EST*	*HU*	*LAT*	*LIT*	*POL*	*ROM*	*SLK*	*SLO*	*Total*
Stock FDI 1998	1,5	14,4	1,8	15,9	1,6	1,6	22,5	4,3	2,5	2,9	69
Potentiel without EU effect	4	12	3	9	2	3	22	7	7	5	74,4
Potentiel with EU effect	7	25	5	18	4	6	42	15	15	10	146,6

Source: Claudia Buch, Robert Kotka et Daniel Piazolo? Does the East Get What Would Otherwise Flow to the South? FDI Diversion in Europe, Kiel Institute of World Economics WP No. 1061

The Initial Effects of FDI on Industrial Restructuring

In the context of *greenfield* investments, the technical and managerial know-how is rapidly transmitted to the staff and labour.

35. Claudia M. Buch, Robert M. Kokta, Daniel Piazolo, 'Does the East Get What Would Otherwise Flow to the South? FDI Diversion in Europe', Kiel Institute of World Economics, *Kiel Working Paper No. 1061*, July 2001.

Unlike a joint venture, the technological appropriation potential moves outside the enterprise, as a result of sub-contracting or imitation by local enterprises, i.e. the so-called national enterprises. As mentioned earlier, firms controlled by foreign capital henceforth represent a significant part of the sales and exports of the manufacturing sector of the CEEC : 25 per cent to 70 per cent and 35 per cent to 90 per cent respectively. In certain sectors, production by local firms is only marginal : 5, 10 and 20 per cent for vehicle engines in Hungary, Poland and the Czech Republic respectively ; a small percentage in the tobacco industry, which ever the country ; 5 to 20 per cent in the paper industry and its derivatives in Poland and Estonia, and only 20 per cent in the radio-television field in Poland and Hungary (40 per cent in the Czech Republic).

The international sector is drawing an increasing share of profits, which is vastly different from the domestic firms. This situation is most noticeable in the Czech Republic and Poland where the ratio of profits to sales in the domestic sector has fallen from 13 to 0.2 per cent and from 4.8 to 1.3 per cent respectively between 1994 and 1998. Several small and medium enterprises do not have the required size to take advantage of the tax incentives proposed by the government (see chapter 6).

If the competitive pressure by foreign firms has weakened the local fabric, some enterprises nevertheless have benefited from the positive externalities created by the change in the business environment and the inflow of FDI. This especially refers to the local sub-contractors working for multinationals, who have had to reorganise and develop their direct supply networks. From another angle, we can cite the Videoton case in Hungary. In addition to its sub-contracting activity, Videoton also rents out a part of its industrial complex and its personnel, a legacy of the socialist era, to IBM and Flextronics in particular. It also concerns local firms that have assumed a regional and even an international dimension. Thus, Nowy Styl, a chair manufacturer established in the Low-Carpates region of Poland, exports from Argentina, *via* Ukraine, to Germany, thanks to the experience acquired by the two founder-brothers of this company earlier in New York. Viisnurk, an Estonian firm specialising in the manufacture of wood products, which once sold skis to the Russians, is also a successful example of conversion. It is now supplying to Ikea, Atomic and Rossignol. The quasi-billionaire Tofan in Romania started his empire by recycling used tires for the local market, of which he eventually gained more than 70 per cent control.

We can also mention local firms with a strong competitive edge, or those that were benefiting from the indirect support of their governments (taxation, non-reimbursable or non-reimbursed loans) and were able to develop internationalisation strategies at the regional level while maintaining a majority of national shareholders. It is not a very common case but which concerns, in particular, the Hungarian oil company MOL, which tried to buyout a major Polish oil group while it was being privatised. It is now making great strides in Romania, Slovakia, Slovenia and Croatia.

Foreign investments have thus led to a dual process of destruction and development of the productive capacities. In terms of direct and indirect employment (sub-contracting) *Greenfield* investments rapidly generates new industrial activities. On the other hand, acquisitions generally lead to immediate and massive lay-offs in the permanent workforce, although workers may be recruited again later. The consequence of this was the overall drop in the workforce of the acquired enterprises, especially in the over-staffed industrial sectors of all the East European countries. The intensity of this rise in unemployment depended on the force of the process of integration and the volume of FDI. As such the unemployment rate was low in Hungary and the Czech Republic, but much more intense in Poland and Slovakia.

FDI, Bridging the Productivity Gap and Setting the Successful Tempo of Convergence

The global impact of foreign investment in the more advanced countries, indicates the dynamic role that it plays in investment and the rapidity and sustainability of growth, thanks in particular to the productivity gains that it generates in the entire economy. The place of FDIs in the CEEC economies reached very significant levels in the early years of the 21st century. From a purely macroeconomic point of view, the two most characteristic ratios are the proportion of FDIs in investment (FDI/GFAF)[36] and above all the accumulated FDI stock

36. Where gross fixed asset formation (GFAF) corresponds to net investment (increase in the paid up capital) + amortisation (renewal of production facilities, i.e. plant and equipment).

as a percentage of GDP. We can indeed consider the latter as a highly productive capital stock that generates an even more effective growth than the stock of average capital.[37] In relation to both criteria, the CEEC seem to be the best placed among the emerging countries, even Bulgaria, which went through a phase of great instability in the initial stages of transition.

The contribution of FDI to annual investment exceeds one fifth of the total productive effort and is nearly half the level in three major economies of the southern Latin American zone (Argentina, Brazil, Chile). It is clearly much higher than in the three South European economies and slightly higher than the Asian economies currently experiencing rapid growth. Only the Irish configuration, where the FDIs represent nearly 90 per cent of manufacturing investment, is an exception among the CEEC. This is important to know, as the Celtic model is the only one to have bridged the gap and caught up with the average standard of living of the EU in less than thirty years.

In the period 1995-2000, Slovakia had a low FDI level, but in 2000 and 2001, suddenly the FDI quantum shot up to 35-40 per cent of the GFAF. The second country to have hit a low was Slovenia, and the statistical correction taking into account the profits re-invested in the country was not enough to enhance the weight of the FDI beyond 5-10 per cent of the GFAF. Two special features of the Slovenian model stand out here : a level of development obviously higher than the average which makes bridging the gap from the outside less necessary; a small country's resolve to promote its domestic enterprises once their average competitiveness level has become satisfactory. This is precisely what happened in some cases, as for example the firm Gorenje[38] (electrical appliances), which exports to the whole of Europe.

In terms of accumulated stock, that is in terms of the average age of this capital (the 1990-1999 variation gives the percentage of capital which is less than ten years old), the CEEC picture looks even

37. Here we are referring to the Harrod-Domar growth model. According to this model, growth $g = K/v$ where K is the stock of capital and v the marginal coefficient of capital or the marginal growth of capital necessary for a 1 per cent increase of GDP.

38. For a detailed description of the originality of the Slovenian model see *Economic Survey of Europe 2001*, United Nations Economic Commission for Europe (UNECE), Geneva.

more promising. On average, the accumulated stock is more than a quarter of the GDP and is less than ten years old, which brings it closer to the Irish case. Two groups actually make their appearance. The first includes three countries (Estonia, Czech Republic, Hungary) and is situated in the 40-50 per cent range, i.e. among the highest levels in the world, for example, Ireland and South East Asia (Malaysia, Thailand). The second is composed of 5 countries (Bulgaria, Latvia, Lithuania, Poland and Romania) and falls in the 15-30 per cent range, i.e. in the same bracket as the South European countries or the Maghreb, with however the advantage of equipment which is three times newer than for example in Spain. Why is this so important?

The evolution of productivity and, in particular, the impact of FDI on it, seems to be the key variable in the catching-up process adopted by the Central and East European countries. In the classic typology of factors of production necessary for growth, the CEEC cannot count quantitatively either on the growth of their working population, like the young Asian countries, or on the abundance of natural resources (like Russia), nor on an increase in the domestic savings (Asia). Their sole driving force in order to catch-up is the more efficient use of their human resources, and a surplus of foreign savings attracted by the higher returns on capital, precisely because of the previous slowdown in the productivity of these countries. And this is what is happening.

The comparison between the level of value added in foreign capital supported enterprises and the value added in domestic enterprises shows that the productivity in the foreign enterprises in the manufacturing sector is on the whole three times higher than in enterprises financed by domestic capital. In evolutionary terms, the annual productivity gains in comparison to the EU15 are some 7 to 10 points more and two to five times higher than the local enterprises. At this rate, we should be able to observe the initial effects of a productivity differential of this magnitude, especially in countries having benefited from large FDI inflows.

Besides the technical and managerial know-how, FDI brings in another essential factor of productivity gains : the greater specialisation of often narrow economies, previously capable of self-sufficiency, but unproductively. This impacts at two levels depending on the source of foreign investment : territorial specialisation but also a more effective specialisation of enterprises.

The sector-wise distribution of FDI supports the thesis of the strong and simultaneous presence of geographically close investors and investors from far off countries, who try to compensate for the competitive handicap of their remoteness. Apart from competition between two groups of actors from the same sector of activity (Volkswagen against Renault), the recipient countries also benefit from the competitive edge provided by the second group of outsiders. In the case of the Central and East European countries, neighbouring countries, such as the Nordic nations, Germany and Italy share their state-of-the-art know-how in electronics, furniture, mechanics and textiles and leather goods. However, the more distant investors, like France and the United States (USA), come and compete with them in the same sectors, for strategic reasons of the offensive or defensive conquest of markets, and bring with them their own centres of excellence. In particular this occurs in the service industry, with its preponderant weight in the FDI inflows to the CEEC (more than 50 per cent) and whose productivity gains are often under-estimated for themselves and for the entire economy. Here, we refer in particular to the modern retail sector (see *infra*), but also Banks. The consequence of this structural mutation is the rapid rise in productivity in the candidate countries, thus ensuring, in all probability, the rapid convergence of these new members of the EU. We must signal, however, the considerable disparity in the catching-up process during the period 1993-1997, and especially the marginalisation of Bulgaria, but also the slow progress made by Slovenia and Romania. What is important, however is the level achieved and the dynamics set in motion. Slovenia already has the highest level of productivity in the region. Romania too has definitely taken off, although a bit late. Bulgaria will probably soon be on the upswing. This is what justifies the importance given by the European Commission to the accession of these two countries, planned for 2007.

The Consumption-Distribution Synergy

The retail sector in central Europe has gone through a transformation in the last ten years the likes of which Europe took

Table 2.4

Sectoral Breakdown of FDI in CEECs (Per cent Total Stock)

	BU*	CZ*	EST**	HU*	LET**	LIT**	POL**	ROU**	SLK**	SLV*
PRIMARY	1.6	1.0	1.5	1.4	1.2	0.0	0.3	3.0	1.4	0.0
Agriculture. hunting and fishing	0.2	0.2	1.2	0.9	0.7	0.0	0.1	3.0	0.2	0.0
Mining and quarrying	1.4	0.9	0.3	0.5	0.5	0.0	0.2	0.0	1.2	0.0
SECONDARY	49.4	45.8	22.8	37.3	17.1	30.0	49.2	43.8	49.1	51.5
Food products and beverages	21.5	7.1	0.0	9.0	5.3	17.0	13.1	13.9	0.0	5.0
Textile-wearing apparel and dressing of furn.	1.0	1.6	0.0	1.6	2.1	0.7	0.7	3.5	0.0	1.1
Wood-publishing and printing	2.1	4.8	0.0	1.8	2.5	0.0	5.7	0.0	0.0	10.9
Coke and petroleum products	0.0	1.6	0.0	0.0	0.0	12.9	0.0	0.0	0.0	0.0
Chemicals and chemical products	4.6	2.4	0.0	8.9	2.7	1.7	3.7	0.0	0.0	7.6
Rubber and plastic products	0.5	2.3	0.0	0.0	0.4	0.0	1.3	0.0	0.0	5.5
Other non-metallic mineral products	0.0	9.5	0.0	2.3	0.9	1.5	5.9	0.0	0.0	3.4
Metal products	8.4	3.4	0.0	3.0	1.9	0.0	1.1	0.0	0.0	2.2
Machinery and equipment	0.0	1.5	0.0	10.3	0.9	0.0	1.5	26.4	0.0	5.1
Electrical machinery and apparatus n.e.c.	1.3	4.5	0.0	0	0.4	1.8	3.6	0.0	0.0	4.1
Motor vehicles	0.9	7.0	0.0	0	0.1	0.8	12.5	0.0	0.0	6.7
Other and Recycling	0.0	0.1	0.0	0.3	0.0	0.0	0.0	0.0	0.0	0.0
TERTIARY	49.0	53.2	75.2	61.4	72.7	35.0	50.5	53.1	49.5	48.5
Electricity-gas and water	0.0	4.7	1.8	17.3	2.6	0.0	1.3	0.0	0.5	0.4
Construction	1.3	1.0	1.0	1.6	0.3	0.0	5.5	2.3	0.0	0.2

Contd...

...Table 2.4 Contd...

	*BU**	*CZ**	*EST***	*HU**	*LET***	*LIT***	*POL***	*ROU***	*SLK***	*SLV**
Wholesale. Retail Trade & repairs of motor vehicles	23.0	17.3	15.7	10.6	16.3	0.6	9.7	24.1	0.0	16.8
Hotels and restaurants	2.1	0.1	1.0	1.8	1.4	0.0	1.2	0.8	18.7	0.6
Transport. storage and communication	5.0	9.2	26.6	8.2	24.9	29.4	5.4	2.3	1.2	1.8
Financial intermediation and insurance	11.4	14.8	23.5	10.9	18.9	5.0	22.4	0.0	3.1	15.4
Real estate-renting and bussiness activity	5.4	5.5	5.0	9.4	7.4	0.0	0.5	0.0	20.3	12.3
Public administration-health and social services	0.0	0.5	0.1	0.1	0.6	0.0	4.5	0.0	3.5	0.9
Other community and social services	0.0	0.0	0.6	1.4	0.3	0.0	0.0	0.0	0.0	0.1
Other services	0.8	0.1	0.0	0.0	0.0	0.0	0.0	23.6	0.3	0.0
UNSPECIFIED	0.0	0.0	0.5	0.0	9.0	35.0	0.0	0.0	0.0	0.0
TOTAL	**100**	**100**	**100**	**100**	**100**	**100**	**100**	**100**	**100**	**100**

twenty-five years to go through. Starting with the assumption that these countries will catch-up with the consumption levels existing in the EU, the commercial revolution has greatly stimulated the retail sector by modernising the logistical and supply channels. There is also a move to homogenise consumer behaviour, although, like Western Europe, significant differences continue to subsist between CEE countries. The result of this consumption and distribution revolution is clearly a better allocation of investment, particularly those who are attracted by these new expanding markets in Europe. But this represent also the guarantee of a better social and cultural homogenisation within Europe, a strong pre-condition of the stated objective of its founding fathers : peace. The comparison with the level and structure of consumption in France and Portugal nevertheless shows that the time factor should be taken into consideration : the consumer revolution has only just begun and will probably continue for at least a decade in the more advanced countries and for much longer in those that are lagging behind Representing nearly 10 per cent of the EU15 retail sales,[39] the stakes are too important and cannot be ignored.

The Rise in Consumption Levels Since the Mid-nineties

After a drop in the early nineties, retail sales in the CEEC experienced a real upswing between 1993 and 1999, depending on the country. From 1993 to 2000, retail sales in current Euros practically doubled in the region as against +25 per cent in EU15. This trend was partly because of the increase in the volume of sales and partly because of the rise in unit values, thus also denoting a change in the nature of the products consumed. The appreciation in the exchange rates of these countries has in fact facilitated the import of a wider range of products, such as cars or electronic goods, which are sold at international prices, unlike several consumer products that are still produced locally and generally sold at much lower prices. Thanks to this phenomenon, the relative weight of retail sales in the region, excluding automobiles, has gone up from 7 per cent of the EU15 sales in 1996 to nearly 10 per cent today.

---

39. In terms of the standard of purchasing power (SPA), in other words taking into account the price differences between different markets for the same products.

This swift recovery, however, has not been homogenous. The retail sector in Slovenia, Poland, Slovakia and Croatia has experienced highs above the average for the CEEC. On the other hand, Romania has regressed relatively and Hungary has undergone a decade small upward variation of 14 per cent before the upswing of the last few years (+12.5 per cent retail sales in 2002). In Hungary this revival was due to a major hike in salaries that the authorities decided upon in 2000 (minimum wage was doubled), in order to redistribute the fruits of the effort put in by the country after the 1995 austerity drive. Each country is allowed to catch-up with the consumption levels of EU15 at its own pace and according to its success in the transition process, as well as according to the choice of distribution of the fruits of growth. Nevertheless, there is a difference between countries in which mass retailing started in 1996 (Hungary, Czech Republic and Poland) and those in which it is still in the embryonic stage. However market penetration of mass retailing seems to be gaining in the entire region, whether it is the provincial towns or countries where the impact until now has been minor, such as Romania. There is an absolute craze in Romania for consumer goods of foreign origin since 2001. This is also the year that the first Carrefour department store was opened in Bucharest.

Disparities between and within the CEEC Countries

Retail sales in Central and Eastern Europe in 2000 represented nearly 170 billion in current Euros, which is small compared to the retail sales in EU15, amounting to approximately 2100 billion in the same year (8 per cent, automobiles included). For all that, each country in the CEEC does not carry the same weight. Expressed in current Euros, retails sales in Poland represented 16.3 per cent of the French sales in 1999, they were 4.3 per cent and 3.6 per cent respectively in the Czech Republic and Hungary, 2 per cent in Slovenia and Romania, while Croatia and Bulgaria represented less than 1 per cent.

Expressed in terms of comparable domestic prices, or standard of purchasing power (SPP), the percentages however change substantially. The Polish retail market thus represents 36 per cent of French sales. This matches estimates by retail professionals, who compare Warsaw and its suburbs with the Lille-Roubaix-Tourcoing region. Sales in the Czech Republic amounted to approximately 11 per cent of French sales and the Hungarian sales came to 8.5 per cent. Romania and Bulgaria were the most affected by the gap between their domestic prices and the level prevailing in the EU15 with the Romanian sales representing actually 8 per cent of the French retail sales, and Bulgarian around 3 per cent. Hence, measured in terms of domestic prices, the total sales of the countries in question represent nearly three-fourths of the French retail sales, i.e. a level that better explains the aggressive strategy of mass retailers in markets that are still considered untouched. And to profit fully from the the volume effect, this big companies like Carrefour and Tisco exercised their full ingenuity in the recent years to find local and regional suppliers whose prices were affordable.

The ratio of the retail sales turnover to population of each country, enables us to identity more distinctly the nature of the opportunities offered by these markets : some offer a greater trade potential than others. We know that the critical thresholds of 5000 and 10,000 Euros per annum and per household are a trigger factor for the purchase of a washing machine or a car respectively . For example, Slovenia accounts for the largest per capital sales : 6912 Euros in terms of SPP against an average 4150 for the region. Poland, Hungary, Czech Republic and Slovakia post a roughly equivalent volume, around 4500-5500 Euros in terms of SPP.

These averages, however, mask great disparities of potential within the candidate countries. Not only are sales in the Greater Budapest region (7.1 billion Euros) the highest as compared to other regions within the CEEC zone, they also easily outdistance the six other Hungarian regions. In 1999, Greater Budapest had 27 per cent of the shops and 41 per cent of the retail outlets in the country as against 12 per cent and 15 per cent respectively in the two Northern and Central Hungarian regions (Eszak Magyarorszàg and Közép Dunàntùl, with 2.1 and 2.6 billion Euros respectively). The Hungarian capital is probably an exception by way of the magnitude of the imbalance, but we find the same disparity between urban and rural consumption zones, between capitals and provinces, especially in Poland, Slovakia and Romania. The average salary in Warsaw is thus two to three times higher than in the provinces. The recent move to open hyper markets in the provinces and introduce measures to boost investment in depressed zones could, however, contribute to the stabilisation of this disparity by staggering the catching up process among the different zones, according to the model developed by Lucas on unequal regional development.[40]

Highly stratified consumption structures as well as the hypertrophy of the foods category, the sector-wise breakdown of retail sales highlights the preponderance of the Automobile category (including spare parts, fuel accessories) – 25 per cent on an average – and the household Furniture-equipment category, especially in Hungary, Czech Republic and Slovenia (18.4, 17.5 and 13.5 per cent respectively). This trend is borne out in Hungary, which was lagging considerably in this field and where the automobile category progressed by more than 12 per cent in 2001, to represent 29 per cent of total sales. The furniture category grew by 40 per cent, reflecting the structural dimension of the catching-up process. It is not so much an increase in value than we are concerned with here, but the convergence of the structure of consumption with West Europe.

The structure of household expenditure in the CEEC, in 1999 is still characterized by the predominance of food products, although considerable divergences reflect very different standards of living. Slovenians thus devote 29.2 per cent of their budget to feed themselves (24 per cent in France), against 35 per cent in Hungary and Poland and more than 53 per cent in Romania. These percentages are comparable to that of France in 1960 (36 per cent) or Spain in 1980 30 per cent). The proportion spent on food should, however, continue to come down under the combined effect of greater competition between the agro-foods enterprises and the development of supermarkets that undoubtedly help to lower prices in this sector, as well as the gradual increase in purchasing power.

Despite the reputation of the communist regime providing almost free housing, housing frequently rank second after food, on the list of household expenses in the CEEC. Hungary (22 per cent) and the Czech Republic (20 per cent) spend considerably on this head, in fact nearly as much as France (24.5 per cent in 1999), and it is increasing

40. This model, developed in 1988 by the American economist Robert Lucas, is a fundamental model of formalised research on human capital and growth. See in particular Robert E. Lucas, 'Why Doesn't Capital Flow from Rich to Poor Countries ?', *American Economic Review*, vol. 80, no. 2, May 1990, pp. 92-96.

all over because of the convergence of housing quality and relative prices. Due to the mass privatisation in favour of the actual occupants almost everywhere, sometimes at very cheap prices, there is in particular 90 per cent of self-owned property in some countries. And they had to bear the burden of the transition after the huge maintenance neglect under the old regime and in the context of rising interest rates. In view of these specifics, housing and its counterpart, housing equipment, represent structurally buoyant markets that large stores, like OBI or Bricorama, lose no time in exploiting.

In the furniture and housing equipment category, purchases are primarily for the purpose of replacement, as the CEEC households were already well equipped. The regional brands of 'white' household appliances of low and medium range, like Görenje, Lehel and Hajdu had gradually penetrated the homes after the Communist regime became more_liberal in the seventies in the aftermath of the Prague spring revolt in 1968. The new purchases concern mainly 'brown' products, with equipment rate much lower than in France for instance (with the exception of television sets). This category will no doubt continue to grow, as the prices of electronics and leisure information technology having fallen, they are now in great demand. During the Communist era they were either inexistent or very expensive because of the technological backwardness of the region.

Transport and communication, which includes Automobiles, automobile accessories and petrol constitute the third expenditure category of households in the CEEC which, in 1999, ranged from 18 per cent in Slovenia (higher than in France, 17.2 per cent) to 13 per cent in Poland, 12 per cent in Hungary and 15 per cent in the Czech Republic. The catching-up phenomenon is obvious : there were 37 cars per 100 households in 1997 and 57 in 1999 in Hungary, even if the vehicular stock continues to be old (between 10 and 14 years, depending on the country). The quantitative and qualitative gap remains important in relation to France, where the equipment rate is 79.4 cars for 100 households. The lure of the latest West European models and the considerably lower prices are some of the reasons for the increasing number of purchases in the last few years. Much more than that, this category along with the mobile (phone) telephony category, correspond perfectly to the needs of consumers, who have become very concerned about their social status, a trend that can be seen in all the Central and East European countries. In this sense they should constitute sustainable buoyant markets.

The health and cosmetics category presents a disparate picture from country to country. It constitutes, for example, a relatively significant share (6 per cent) and a growing one in Poland and the Czech Republic. However, disparities are mainly due to the price of medicines and the very different modes of reimbursement from one country to another. But also because of the special articulation of the corporal relationship that varies culturally between countries, as the representatives of L'Oréal, the cosmetics firm, observed during their operations in the zone. This category should normally continue to grow because of the increasing importance of hygiene and physical appearance and also because of the structure of the age pyramid : 20 per cent individuals in the age group 60 years and above in 2000 and 34 per cent to 43 per cent, depending on the country, in the year 2050 (based on United Nations forecasts). On the other hand, the youth, who constitute the age group with highest income, and especially young women, continue to live with their parents till very late and are therefore able to spend a large chunk of their salaries on cosmetics. This is also true of Japan.

Expenditure on leisure activities needs special mention. As in France, most countries spend an equivalent amount, around 9-10 per cent on leisure (expenditures), except, in all logic, countries that are lagging the most. Romania and Bulgaria stand out distinctly here (three times less). The the similarity of the expenditure pattern with France of the first group of countries seems less logic, on the other hand, given the income gap of one to three, even if domestic prices are lower. In fact, this is explained by a dual legacy : one, relative expenditure is still very low on housing and automobiles, and two, the rapprochement of the lifestyles between the two parts of Europe despite significant differences in income. To make up for the poor work intensity under communism, leisure was more developed and has automatically remained at this level because of a ratchet-like effect when normally it should have come down. We can see this with regard to holidays which are distinctly longer than those in emerging countries with a comparable standard of living (once again we are referring to Asia). This legacy of central Europe is clearly an *acquis*.

Standardisation and Specificity of Consumption Modes

With regard to trends, a recent sociological study by a communications consultancy firm, EURO RSCG,[41] proposed a two-fold approach in terms of sequencing and types of consumers in the CEEC. From 1990 to 1993, a trend *'West is Best'* came to dominate, with the brand exercising a powerful ideological influence on consumption patterns of the type : *'I consume therefore I am free'*. From 1993 to 1998, the brand acquired social connotations : *I consume therefore I am*, and signaled the emergence of a new middle class, the gainers of transition, i.e. young, upwardly mobile white collar citizens (employees, intermediary professions and business executives), etc. On the other hand, since 1998, there has been an about turn with the slogan: *'I compare before consuming'*. The brand continues to be social, but already there is a gradual saturation of supply. As a result local brands acquire a new status : a new found independence and a capacity to exist on their own in the new Europe.

With regard to types of consumers, EURO RSCG distinguishes two categories. In the first category are the trend setters, the youth, first generation consumers, the women who create the consumption modes, and lastly, the entrepreneurs-managers, sensitive to novelty, the consumers of services, who trigger the new trends. The second category is composed of the more traditional mentalities, between 22 per cent and 30 per cent of the population, according to countries, i.e. probably as many in number as the trend setters.

We find these observations in the studies conducted by the German competitor of RSCG, GfK. In Hungary, for example, GfK distinguishes five groups with differing lifestyles whose breakdown is as follows : in the 14-24 age group, there are 14 per cent losers (mainly boys living in small towns, blue collar workers and in a difficult financial situation); on the opposite side, a group of hedonists of similar strength (also boys, 17-20 years of age and living mainly in Budapest); the upwardly mobile individuals are more numerous (30 per cent), mostly women, educated and living in provincial towns; on the opposite side are to be found a group of traditionalists (24 per cent), women being the majority, but living in

41. This communications firm appeared in the market immediately after the demise of the Berlin Wall. It has become one of the top firms in the region and has a regional office in Prague.

villages on slender resources ; lastly, a group of new-comers representing approximately one in five young persons, composed mainly of educated boys from rich families.

Table 2.5

Households Disposal of Consumer Durable Goods in CEECs, France and Portugal

	Bulgaria 1999	*Czech R. 1998*	*Hungary 1999*	*Poland 1999*	*Romania 1999*	*Slovenia 1999*	*Portugal 1996*	*France 1999*
Freezer	na	53	67	41.3	41.3	84	51	47
Microwave	na	28	60	13.9	14	20	17.3	51
Color TV	80	99	93	95	95.5	93	94.4	97
Videotape	na	38	71	56.6	56.6	42	52	65
Computer	na	20	19	11.5	11.5	21	18	23
Dishwasher	na	4	2	1.1	1.1	21.8	18.4	38
Videocamera	na	5	5	3	3	6	8	14
Car*	21.9	33.9	21.9	23.0	12.5	41.0	75.0	80.0
Mobile*	3	18.9**	30	17.2	10	55	26	42

* Ratio for 100 people except for France: 100 households ** 1999.

Source: Countries official data.

Despite recent developments, these markets have not become homogeneous in relation to each other. The recent evolution in the purchasing patterns of food products observed in Hungary, Poland, the Czech Republic and Slovakia shows a lack of homogenisation of the consumption patterns. The persistence of structural gaps between these countries is due to the great number of constituents in the domestic economy and, in particular, the degree of motorization of households and the level of professional activity of women. The analysis shows that the use of the car and frequent visits to shopping malls go hand in hand. They are part of the same technological choice, aimed at economising time, a factor that is all the more important in view of the temporal constraints that women in particular have. We could also integrate into this analysis the influence of cultural factors, measured by the utility function associated with domestic activity, in this case the purchase of food products, for this varies with each type of consumer. A country like Hungary stands out because of the proportionate increase in the neighbourhood options in the strict sense of the term (traditional shops and mini markets) as well as in the broad sense (including discount shops). On the whole, perceptible differences in the structures of the shopping options in the entire region surprise those who were banking on the homogenisation of the behaviour patterns in these economies. Each market thus requires a subtle approach taking into account the degree of convergence with the West European lifestyles, the specific history of transition in each country and, lastly, the sociological structures that are unique to each one.

3

Trade as a Means of European Integration

Broadly speaking, in just a few years, most CEE countries have become small, specialised and very open economies. From one star-shaped structure stretching West-East around Russia, they now form several star-shaped structures East-West around the principal proximity centres of the European Union, such as the Nordic countries, Germany and Italy. This new blueprint is indicative of a possible reinforcement of the regional sub-basins in Greater Europe, a process that may well take twenty years and more to complete. The one certainty is that the new Europe will not much resemble the Europe that we are familiar with once the integration of the twelve, thirteen or more new members of the Union has been completed.

Normalisation of Trade and Geographical Reorientation

Rapid Trade Liberalisation, a Powerful Instrument of Transition

The shock of transition was cushioned by the rapidity with which trade adjustment took place. While the CEECs' GDP index fell in 1990 and did not recover to its 1989 level until 2000, there was a systematic upswing of the trade indexes throughout the entire decade. The exports from Central and Eastern Europe more or less tripled in value, but in terms of volume they more than quadrupled, thus invalidating the pessimistic theories put forward by some experts who were sceptical about the capacity of the Eastern productive machinery to reorient itself. The Association Agreements signed almost immediately with the European Union resulted in liberalising the trade of manufactured goods as early as 1991-1992 (see chapter 1). But trade liberalisation was even quicker with regard to imports: the index went up to nearly 350 in 2001, whereas the export index was less than 300 (base 100 in 1990). This phenomenon resulted in a sort of accelerated adjustment of the productive machinery. On the one hand, imported consumer goods competed with local products, even the very cheap ones, despite the sharp fall of CEECs' currencies at the beginning of the transition process. This forced domestic supply to adapt very quickly. This meant that more and more modern inputs[42] were imported, enabling East European exports to become qualitatively competitive. The switch to the practice of sub-contracting in textiles, leather and furniture is a good example (see *infra*).

The trade deficit that resulted from this asymmetric dynamism between imports and exports was synonymous with a huge current account imbalance of the in several countries, as it systematically exceeded 5 per cent of GDP and at times even touched 8-9 per cent, for example in Slovakia in 2002. However, in the case of the CEECs, financing the trade_deficit has never been a major constraint thanks to the substantial pre-accession financial aid from the EU and to a general atmosphere of confidence among bankers. In this context, we may recall for example the re-negotiation of the Polish external debt in 1992, which preceded the boom in the mid-nineties in that country. It was the regular direct investment flows that very rapidly financed this import-driven growth, whether it was for procuring inputs used in the production of export goods or, increasingly so, equipment for modernising existing plants or establishing new ones.

The external deficits would have immediately become unmanageable if the CEEC exports had not been able to keep up with the momentum because of the loss of competitiveness or the wrong choice of specialisation. The Polish example since 2000 illustrates that drastic economic policies have to be adopted, even if the consequence is the slowdown or the decline of growth. The issue of Central Europe trade competitiveness is thus at the heart of their successful integration into Europe, as also it is for the necessary adaptation of the old 15 Member States.

Trade liberalisation did not merely sustain the first steps of the transition process, it also normalised the economies of Central and Eastern Europe. The opening up rate of trade in these formerly closed economies, but which had started to open up during the eighties, began to progress very quickly, in conformity with the European blueprint for greater sectoral and geographical specialisation of the small economies.

42. Factors that go into the production of a good (eg. energy, fertilisers and agricultural inputs).

Table 3.1

Trade Opening Intensity for CEECs (Export+Import)/GDP at Current Exchange Rate)

	1990	1991	1992	1993	1994	1995	1996	1997	1998	1999	2000	2001
Bulgaria	28	66	95	77	85	85	102	97	76	77	94	93
Czech R.	45	64	63	75	71	90	86	94	97	102	120	117
Estonia	58	122	110	113	130	122	105	154	153	112	149	138
Hungary	50	55	53	50	60	63	65	88	104	109	124	128
Latvia	9	12	129	100	62	73	70	76	81	69	71	71
Lithuania	9	9	111	156	98	102	101	99	88	73	82	88
Poland	48	33	33	34	39	41	43	47	47	43	51	45
Romania	22	29	51	41	42	51	55	56	48	53	63	61
Slovakia	80	112	90	94	92	95	101	91	112	109	141	136
Slovenia	51	63	101	97	97	95	93	97	97	92	104	102
CEEC10	39	43	55	57	58	63	64	70	71	71	82	78
EU15	44,2	41,7	40,4	40	42	45	45	48	49	49	48	47

Official sources

Figure 3.1

Trade Flows and GDP Indexes During the Post-Communist Transition (100 in 1990)

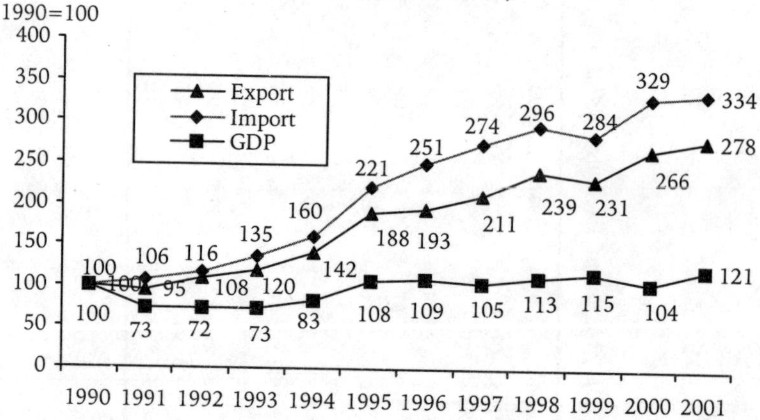

Official Sources

Whether it involves measuring the GDP at the current exchange rate or on the basis of purchasing power parity in order to take lower domestic prices into account, it is incontestable that the CEE economies have opened up considerably in just a few years. In fact, the trade/GDP ratio (X + M/GDP)[43] has taken less than ten years to double. This phenomenon is not even remotely the logical result of the fall in production levels that occurred at the beginning of the decade. The monetary value of the trade flows has in fact tripled from 50 to more than 150 billion dollars in either direction. The average opening up rate of the region is henceforth around 70-80 per cent, i.e. much more than the European Union average, but perfectly comparable with the small economies (i.e. Netherlands at 87 per cent) whose GDP in current values is perfectly comparable with the aggregate GDP of the CEE applicant countries. The smallest economies such as the Baltic States have exceeded the opening up ratio of 150 per cent for goods alone. The small countries, with a population of 5 to 10 million inhabitants, have a ratio between 100 and 120 per cent. The bigger countries such as Poland or Romania

43. Where X represents exports and M imports.

are slightly above 50 per cent. That is at the same level as Spain (41 per cent, but more than 50 per cent if we include services such as tourism).

This scenario is in conformity with the principle of the greater specialisation of territories in the larger economic Union. We can expect growth gains from this blueprint in terms of a more efficient allocation of the factors of production, especially through the production concentration mechanism of increasing returns, but also through a better exploitation of the classic comparative advantages of each part of the Union. The study of the modifications of the geographical and sectoral structures will help to specify the various forms of this new CEEC specialisation.

The Re-direction of Trade Flows Towards the European Union will Continue

In terms of the geographical orientation of trade, the CEEC external trade changed tack in the nineties from the East to the West, but regional trade (European) nevertheless remained paramount. Trade with the rest of the world, especially the United States and Asia, was and still remains marginal. With the former USSR it declined sharply and is now very marginal. Inversely, the EU15 and intra-CEEC trade aggregate amounts to more than three-fourths of the trade these countries were engaged in at the beginning of the year 2000. However, the expected asymmetry between the periphery, involved in the catching up process, and the EU15 is obvious : although the CEE countries have in just a few years become as important in terms of trade as the Iberian peninsula, their weight for EU15 remains marginal and unlikely to bring about fundamental localization changes within Greater Europe.

We cannot say that in the early 2000s the reorientation of trade towards the European Union had been completed. According to the economists using gravitational models[44] to predict the levels and the geographical structure of trade, the progress margin of exports by the candidate countries towards the European Union was very significant in 1997. However, as per the econometric model used, their average

44. Vincent Aussiloux, Michaël Pajot, 'Enjeux commerciaux de l'élargissement de l'Union européenne', working paper, Minefi, Forecasts Division, Paris 2001.

export level was in fact a mere 35 per cent approximately of their estimated potential. Above all, while most EU countries were achieving their potential level, the catching-up by the CEECs was still very unequal at the time of the study. Among the candidate countries, Hungary occupied a special position. In fact, it had more or less attained its potential trade level with the EU as far back as 1997 : nearly 100 per cent of its potential import level and 80 per cent of its potential export level. It is the only country in the group to have achieved these levels. The indifferent performance of the other candidate countries *vis-à-vis* the EU once again shows the poor adaptation to European demand as well as a lack of mastery of techniques and of marketing networks. In fact, the Hungarian example is instructive for it was the first to have privatised its economy. It is also the only country where the foreign enterprises' share in its total exports exceeds 80 per cent. Many of its investors are multinationals that have chosen to establish their manufacturing bases in Hungary in fields such as electronics, automobiles (motors), pharmaceuticals and agro-foods. The same scenario can be found in Ireland where, in the field of information technology, the major American multinationals decided in the eighties to profit from the

Table 3.2

The New Geographical Trade Patterns of CEECs 1992-2000

(Per cent)

	1992 Exports	*2000 Exports*	*1992 Imports*	*2000 Imports*
Total	100	100	100	100
EU15	59	65	56	62
North America	3	5	6	2
Developped Asia	1	1	3	1
Eastern Europe	15	18	16	12
Former USSR	4	3	5	11
Dev Asia	4	2	4	6
Latin America	2	1	2	1
Middle East	7	3	5	1
Others	4	3	4	3

Source: FMI DOTS

advantages offered by the Dublin authorities to establish a base for exports to the EU.

In the case of the other CEE countries, the delay in applying this strategy in the nineties resulted in a poorer penetration of the European markets than expected in view of their per capita GDP level, their geographical distance from the Union or the size of their economy. These results were corroborated in an important study[45] on the subject conducted by the National Bank of Hungary. But in view of the evolution of direct investment and Poland's difficult economic situation, which had been counting on the advantages of its domestic market to attract FDI, it is possible that imports by the EU from the candidate countries will henceforth increase more quickly than their exports to these countries. In this context, the earlier enlargements can serve as a comparison and provide two typical scenarios depicting the evolution of trade between the CEECs and the EU15.

There were relative economic similarities that characterised the more advanced CEE countries as well as Greece and Portugal before accession (low per capita GDP and especially labour costs). This combined with the evolution of the trade potential's coverage ratio of Greece and Portugal since their entry into the EU, can help us to draw some lessons on the prospects of external trade for the candidate countries once they become part of the EU. We can in particular distinguish two contrasting trajectories, which probably correspond to two typical scenarios available to the future Member States, if we exclude the previously cited Irish example:

1) Since its accession in 1981, Greek exports to the EU have paradoxically covered an increasingly smaller segment of the potential level (from 54 per cent to 39 per cent). At the same time the coverage ratio of the potential exports of the EU to Greece also declined (from 115 per cent to 105 per cent). Thus, even if trade between the EU and Greece expanded considerably in this period, its progression turned out to be much less than what was expected of this country

45. Zoltán M. Jakab, Mihály A. Kovács, András Oszlay, "How Far Has Trade Integration Advanced ? An Analysis of the Actual and Potential Trade of Three Central and Eastern European Countries", *Journal of Comparative Economics*, Vol. 29, June 2001, pp. 276-292.

in view of its characteristics and its distance from the European Union;

2) At the time of its accession in 1986, Portugal's trade level with the EU was less than its potential level because it was more exposed to extra-European geographical zones, especially its former colonies. One decade after its accession, the situation was reversed. In 1997 Portugal attained 100 per cent of its export potential with the EU as against 71 per cent in 1985. From the point of view of the import trade potential, the latter was 141 per cent in 1997, as against 69 per cent in 1985. Unlike Greece, whose evolution was completely the opposite, Portugal, thus, succeeded in reorienting its trade towards the EU, thereby exceeding the trade levels that, in view of the economic and geographic distances, it would have normally achieved. This also applies to Ireland, but it is even more marked, while Spain is an intermediary position between Portugal and Ireland.

These divergences in the evolution of the trade potential's coverage ratio are certainly one important explanation of the variance in the performance of the two countries with regard to the evolution of their economic growth. Expressed in terms of purchasing power parity, the per capita GDP thus increased by 64 per cent in Portugal between 1985-1999 as against 22 per cent in Greece. From then on it would seem that the capacity of the candidate countries to adopt a Portuguese-type scenario (rapid convergence) rather than a Greek-type scenario and *a fortiori* of course, an Irish scenario, will condition the major part of their economic performances. Just like Hungary and Ireland, one explanation for the difference in performance of Greece and Portugal resides clearly in their very different capacity to attract foreign investments. In particular, we have seen in Chapter 2 that Greece's FDI entry index was situated at a very low level. In fact, not one CEE country is found in this category. All of them are in an index bracket between the Irish and Portuguese scenarios, including Romania and Bulgaria. Trade integration with the EU should therefore continue at a more or less quick pace, varying from country to country.

The Revival of Intra-CEEC Trade: A Crucial Component of the Intra-EU27 Trade

In the beginning of the nineties, trade among the erstwhile COMECON countries fell drastically, not only with Russia but also with each other. To remedy the situation they had to first build a more balanced sectoral and geographical structure from the viewpoint of international market mechanisms. Catching up with the EU, in fact, now became a priority. As the previously mentioned study by the National Bank of Hungary shows, the future of trade relations within the zone also merits a more rigorous examination in the light of the observed facts. To do this, on the technical side we have the same tools that we had in the EU case, i.e. the gravitational models, which link trade intensities with geographical proximity and the relative size of economies. We talk of balanced or optimal integration potential when actual trade corresponds to calculated trade.

What are the observations made by the National Bank of Hungary? With regard to the three large central European countries (Poland, the Czech Republic and Hungary), during the period 1993 to 1997, the Bank concluded that there was still room to achieve an optimal level of trade between the CEFTA countries.[46] With regard to exports, for example, Poland had only achieved half its equilibrium potential, as also in relation to the EU. The same was true of Hungary, which on the other hand had more or less normalized its trade with the EU. Only the Czech Republic was excessively integrated at_the regional level owing to its historical links with Slovakia. It was, in fact, clearly lagging behind the other countries of the region and especially Poland. In short, in 1997, the basic model used by the National Bank of Hungary predicted that trade reorientation would probably play an important role in helping intra-CEEC trade to catch up.

What is the situation currently on this front? As statistics show, the evolution of trade among the central European countries need not feel ashamed of the exceptional progress with the EU zone. Their

46. CEFTA or Central European Free Trade Area, a free trade zone created by the four Visegrad countries (Poland, Czech Republic, Slovakia and Hungary), officially came into being in 1993, and was later joined by several other countries from the region, such as Croatia, in 2001.

Table 3.3

The Intra-CEE Trade Dynamism

Export from—>to	*Per cent in 1993*	*Per cent in 2000*	*2000/1993* (1993=100)
CZ—>HU	2.1	1.9	229
CZ—>POL	2.8	5.8	532
CZ Total export	100	100	252
HU—>CZ	2.0	1.9	306
HU—>POL	1.9	2.6	434
HU Total export	100	100	327
POL—>CZ	2.3	3.7	360
POL—>HU	1.0	2.1	453
POL Total export	100	100	224
Total Intra CEE3	4.0	6.0	390
Total Export CEE3	100	100	259

Source: from DOTS IMF 2002.

growth was 290 per cent between 1993 and 1997 for the three countries under consideration, each of which has roughly the same growth pattern : more than 300 per cent in Poland, +350 per cent in the Czech Republic and +275 per cent in Hungary. In terms of relative weight, cross trade between these three countries, has increased from 4 per cent to 6 per cent of their total trade. If this relative share is still modest, it is because the size of their GDP in comparison with the neighbouring EU15 is only 4-5 per cent at the current rate of exchange. However, recent trends suggest that the current momentum of the inter-regional dynamism will continue in the coming years. Once again one of the reasons is the important role of FDI in the re-organisation of the production systems of the region. Its underlying logic is in fact to create a real process of regional integration in the medium term on the basis of the regional division of labour, both in relation to consumer goods as well as intermediate products, which are contingent on the restrictions imposed by economies of scale, transport costs and country-wise and even region-wise specialisation.

In concrete terms, a car assembly centre exists, for example, in the Czech Republic, but the motors and components are for the most part manufactured in Slovakia, Poland and Hungary. With regard to agro-foods, although tastes differ from country to country, an increasing number of products are labeled in all the Central European languages. They are manufactured in the several dozen Danone and Bongrain factories, to take only the French groups, found all over the region. In the field of electronics, it is the Hungarian and Estonian centres that dominate. Slovakia, for its part, is a major supplier of intermediate goods to the entire CEFTA, and especially steel sheets produced in the famous blast furnaces of Kosice, which were acquired in November 2000 by US Steel. The CEEC markets are still relatively limited and marketing is an important aspect in all of them (or in a maximum viable number). Thus it is completely natural to see an increase in the cross flows. In short, their value and their relative shares are still small, but the trend seems to indicate that sub-regional integration is increasing in the context of the geographical re-organisation of the European continental economy.[47]

CEEC-Russia Trade: Are Legacy and Geographical Proximity an Asset?

After the disintegration of the Comecon and the financial crisis in Russia, what trade still remains between the CEECs and their big neighbour? Do the candidate countries constitute a platform for exports to Russia? What aspects of this trade can complement one another and what would be the choice of specialisation?

In terms of value, exports to Russia have sustained two shocks. The first one occurred between 1989 and 1993, when the combined exports of Poland, ex-Czechoslovakia, Hungary, Romania and Bulgaria fell by half, i.e. from 13 billion dollars to less than 3 billion. After a slight recovery, the 1997 Russian crisis constituted the second shock and between the years 1998-1999 exports again declined. Despite a strong recovery in 2000 (+34 per cent), they are currently a mere one-third of their level prior to the crises, or 2.6 billion as against 8.4 billion dollars for the 12 CEE countries and

---

47. As it so happens this is the conclusion of a market study conducted in 2002 by the author: Boillot J.J. and alii, "New Trade Geography of Eastern Europe," *Economic and Political Weekly* Vol. XXXIX No. 20, May 15-21, 2004, pp. 2001-2004. Online www.epw.org.in

Turkey[48] (CEE13). With regard to imports from Russia, the slight initial decline was the result of a fall in volume but which was compensated by a huge rise in the price of Russian energy, a sector that was heavily subsidised during the COMECON era. The resurgence in the consumption of energy and raw materials in the CEE countries in the mid-nineties helped to maintain regular deliveries towards Central Europe, despite half-hearted attempts at diversification.

In terms of the relative weight for each partner, this trade is hence characterized by an absolute reversal of the previous asymmetry : in 2000, trade with the candidate countries represented 22 per cent of Russian exports, whereas for them the Russian market became marginal, representing a mere 2 per cent of their total sales abroad. Even the great dependence of the CEECs on the Russian energy sector henceforth does not carry much weight in relation to the whole : 9 per cent of their total imports, against 65 per cent from the European Union. But it still corresponds to 5 per cent of their current GDP and therefore constitutes a trade segment that the CEECs cannot afford to ignore.

In terms of export sectors, Russian specialisation in energy remains very significant: its share hardly deviated from 70 per cent of the total import of the former COMECON countries of Europe between 1993 and 1998. On the CEEC side also, there was a certain stability during this period : a little more than 30 per cent of their total agro-foods exports, around 15-20 per cent for the chemical industry, and lastly around 10 per cent for their automobile, mechanical and wood-pulp sectors. To sum up, it was essentially the volumes that were adjusted, while adjustment in the sectoral structures was minor as if the famous 'socialist division of labour' had merely followed the logic of classic comparative advantages !

Can one expect a definite revival of trade in the future? Paradoxically, Russia's share in the CEEC exports in terms of its

48. An Euro-centric reading of the geographical maps prevents us from understanding Turkey's proximity vis-à-vis the former USSR countries. This is not the case with the Turkish official maps. The distance between Istanbul and Moscow is comparable to that between Istanbul and Prague and much less than between Istanbul and the heart of EU15, if we take Brussels as the heart.

weight in the global GDP remains at a relatively high level. The intensity of trade is in effect 2.5 times more than the economic weight of Russia. But its level is the same as between the EU15 and Russia. The two zones have neither the same past nor the same geographical proximity to the Russian market. We can therefore conclude that the immediate proximity of the CEEC does not constitute a specific advantage over the EU15, at least for the moment. The reason seems to stem from two sets of factors : the nature of the Russian demand and the type of specialisation adopted by the CEE countries :

1) The principal exports of the EU15 to Russia are in fact equipments (nuclear reactors, boilers and machines constitute more than 20 per cent), very little of which are being manufactured by the CEECs. But exports also include food items (13 per cent), electric and telecommunication appliances (10 per cent), wood-pulp and furniture (7 per cent), and automobiles (6 per cent), all of which are available in the CEECs and are moreover technologically upgraded by West European firms established in Central Europe. Furthermore, several groups had established themselves in Central Europe in the early stages of transition, electing the CEECs as their base for exports to Russia. For example, medicines were exported from Hungary (Sanofi), furniture and agro-foods from Poland, and cars from the Czech Republic (Volkswagen) and Turkey (Renault and Fiat).
2) With regard to exports from the Central and East European countries to Russia, excepting for capital goods, there is a great structural similarity with the EU sales to Russia. Only country-wise specialisation is more advanced and in general is a continuation of past strengths. For example, Hungary and Poland's forte is food products, with 20 per cent and 40 per cent respectively of the total sales to Russia ; the countries specialising in chemicals and pharmaceuticals are Slovenia (12 per cent), Bulgaria (12 per cent), Hungary (15 per cent) and the Czech Republic. The Czech Republic is equally strong in the mechanical and automotive fields, followed by Hungary in the latter. Lastly, in the wood-pulp

sector, Poland has clearly emerged as the leader (from 14 per cent to 55 per cent). In reality, the similarities between the EU15 and the CEE countries are merely apparent. European products are generally more up-market and include brand names aimed at the rich CIS consumers, whereas the East European products target the middle class consumers. But we also find popular products on the market which, as a result of the 1998 devaluation, are well positioned in terms of price competitiveness including in the CEECs like the Lada cars for example, but also somefood products. This is what explains the decline in Polish sales to Russia after its financial crisis in early 2000 and their recovery when the Russian economy recovered despite the Putin government will to re-industrialise the country whether by explicit or by implicit protective trade measures. This can be seen from the fierce internal debate within the country as to whether Russia should or should not join the World Trade Organisation (WTO).

The prospects of trade with Russia will thus depend on three factors : the strategy adopted by foreign investors on Russian soil, and especially the improvement, if any, brought about in the business climate in the country ; the extent to which Russia plans to liberalise trade in the event of its entry into the WTO ; and lastly, an important point, the future of energy procurement by the CEEC from Europe and its corollary, the opening up of the European energy sector to revamped Russian groups. With regard to the first two aspects, it is difficult to determine at present what direction Russia will choose to take. We can nevertheless assume that Russia will take advantage of the distance effect, the size of its market and will, moreover, not be satisfied with being a mere manager of natural economic rents in order to promote local production with or without the help of transnational firms. This would besides apply to the average and low-end demand segments, while the rest will continue to be imported. Consequently, there is a risk that the complementarity with the CEEC will be reduced except for some special fields, such as pharmaceuticals. On the third point the strategic choices are no where near a decision, as we can see in the CEEC and especially Poland.

Enlargement and the New Economic Geography of Continental Europe

The Premise of a Polymorphous Europe Divided into Regional Belts

The trade liberalisation in the CEEC did not primarily lead to quantitative shortages as the volume of trade involved was small (6-7 per cent of the EU27). It is possible, nevertheless, that its geographical orientation characterized by strong neighbourhood or proximity effects, reinforced the 'basin effects' within Greater Europe. In fact, the regional basin phenomenon can already be seen in the analysis of the relative trade intensities within the EU27 and should result in the transition from a *monocentric* Europe – concentrated around the London-Paris-Frankfurt triangle – to a more *polymorphous* model.[49] Somewhat similar to the way in which American economic geography is structured around major belts, 'high technology clusters'/specialised centres (*Silicon Valley*) and structuring axes, such as Route 128, which connects Boston to New York. The difference is that the European belts, which we are now in a position to better identify, are manifestly less specialised, each one *vis-à-vis* the others, and that trade is becoming increasingly structured by intra-branch trade or a product range. This conclusion partly coincides with the opinion of the American economist Paul Krugman, consulted on this subject some years ago by the European Commission.[50]

All the belts are not subject to the same intensity because of the presence of transition countries on their immediate flank. This is especially true of France and the Iberian Peninsula and in fact, broadly speaking, of the entire Atlantic arc, which is rather apprehensive about being relegated to the sidelines, in other words about becoming 'the forgotten of Europe'[51]. The new markets and the comparative advantages of the CEEC will equally reinforce the economic power and competitiveness of the developed European belts in which they are gradually integrated. This is evident in the case of the Nordi

49. The rather happy expression is used in the European Commission's 2001 Report on Cohesion.

50. On this subject see Paul Krugman, Geography and Trade.

51. Pierre Cherreau, the regional correspondent of the paper Le Monde, used this expression when writing about the Atlantic Arc Commission's (AAC) General Assembly meeting, attended by thirty regions of the western maritime belt (Le Monde, July 4, 2002).

countries, Germany and Italy. It also applies to the extension of Europe's_structuring axes (Paris-Moscow), and to the revival of the old historical axes, for example towards Turkey. In this sense enlargement is not just a question of twelve or twenty new members, but rather it is the qualitative change of the continental European space that is at stake here. An initial assessment of these readjustments can be made from the simple description of the new commercial trade networks that link the actual members of the EU15 to the future members.

As in the case of the trade potential, one of the preferred instruments for identifying the sub-regional integrative spaces are the gravitational models that use the weight of the economies and the physical distances between the partner countries. Their results are quite similar to the picture presented by a simpler statistical index : the relative trade intensities (RTI).[52] The closer the countries are, the stronger are the intensities like in the case of Austria and Germany, or Greece and Italy, or Finland and the two other Nordic countries (Denmark and Sweden). At first glance, this observation is what fuels the assumption according to which the eastward enlargement could shift the Union's centre of gravity towards the German economy, which would then emerge as the big winner. Nevertheless, a more detailed analysis of the geographical structure of the EU27 countries, based on a very disaggregated analysis of the RTI index represented in the form of a radar chart, results in a quite perceptibly different conclusion with no more clear Centre and the outbreak of few basins instead. Moreover, with such a progressive geographical enlargement of the initial European Union, the sub-regional polarities are more and more transcending the simple proximity effect and exhibit what we can call 'regional belt effects'. For instance, despite the distance being equal between Slovenia on one hand and Italy and Germany on the other hand, Italy is economically closer to Slovenia than is Germany. The difference is even more striking in the case of the Scandinavian countries and the Baltic States and is the outcome of a large variety of factors among which history and culture play a central role. These belts, structured

52. The relative trade intensity (RTI) helps to measure the degree of trade proximity of two economies a and b according to the intensity of trade between them. This index is calculated by the formula : RTI = [(X a!b + M a!b) ÷ (X m!m + M m!m)] ÷ [((X a!m + M a!m) x (X b!m + M b!m)) ÷ (X m!m)) ÷ (X m!m)^2] where : a = country a ; b = country b ; m = world ; X = exports and M = imports.

around the principal developed sub-centres, are involved in an ongoing process of extension and reorganisation of the EU economic geography ever since the fall of the Berlin Wall.

The opening up of the CEECs and the very rapid integration of their production systems with the whole, has manifestly reinforced these centres by increasing their economic size and the possibility of a greater division of labour within them, not only horizontally but also vertically because of the very unequal levels of development between the countries which constitute them. The same phenomenon was, at least partially, repeated in East Asia, when the communist countries, such as China, Vietnam and Cambodia, opened up[53]. By expanding decisively the European space (a 30 per cent area increase of the area), the eastern enlargement has fractured the space which was previously much more mono-centric, into five major European zones or regional belts, of which three are directly affected by the eastward enlargement.

The New Economic Geography of Europe: Five Belts and the Two New Expanding Axes

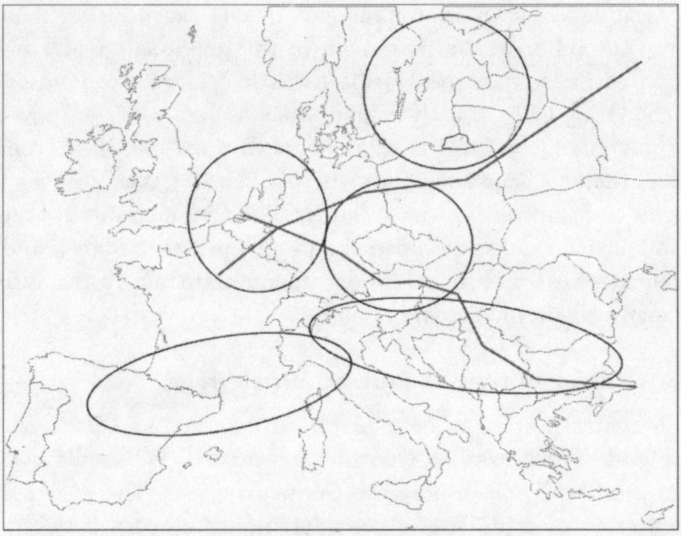

53. Edward Ky Chen, Chi Hung Kwan (dir.), *Asia's Borderless Economy: The Emergence of Subregional Economic Zones*, Paul & Co. Publishers, Hong Kong, 1998, or : J.J. Boillot and N. Michelon, "The South China Triangle and Taiwan, From a Maquilladoras Zone to an Integrated Economy," *China Perspectives No.30*, July-August 2000, p. 32-37. Online www.cefc.com.hk/

The Nordic Basin or the *Mare Balticum*

This belt is emerging distinctly around the Baltic Sea following the integration of the Baltic countries and Poland's maritime frontage with the Nordic economies such as Finland, Sweden and Denmark. The latter's trade zone, in terms of relative intensity, is particularly revealing of a sub-regional bias, which goes beyond the mere distance factor. Denmark, bordering Germany and in a way even Great Britain, has a relative trade intensity that is much more marked with its Baltic neighbours. Another interesting phenomenon, a northern economy as specialised as Finland's (50 per cent of its exports involve electronics and wood products) should, from a strictly theoretical point of view, have a homogeneous relative intensity with all the European countries. An extreme case would be an economy manufacturing just one particular type of furniture, which it would export all over Europe in relatively identical proportions. It is often on the basis of this principle of reinforced specialisation that one can explain how the small economies, Nordic in particular, were the big winners of the single market established in the nineties, with an average growth rate much higher than the European Union's. We have seen in the previous chapter on the origin of FDIs, that the Nordic firms had largely conquered the neighbouring CEECs, both their markets as well as their know-how, and in consequence, had rapidly integrated them into their economic space, thereby benefiting from the market effects as well as from greater competitiveness within Europe. Good examples of this are the Scandinavian banks, omnipresent in all the Baltic States, and the localisation of mobile telephone manufacturing by the Finnish company Nokia, in Estonia.

The Central European Belt or *Mitteleuropa*

A central European belt, historically known as *Mitteleuropa*, is clearly identifiable around Germany and Austria. We should however be careful when examining the German regions. The geographical orientation of trade shows considerable differences between, for example, Bavaria, wholly aligned with its Eastern flank, Hesse manifestly much more aligned with the North European triangle, and lastly Hamburg, which already had serious links with the Baltic region. We do not know at this stage how enlargement will affect the degree of integration of the German *Länders* and if we can continue to perceive Germany as an integrated centre in its own right or as several centres that are integrated with the various European belts. This is obviously the case of France (see *infra*).

This reservation made, in the context of this study we choose to treat Germany as a homogeneous whole, with the *Mitteleuropa* area outlined on the radar chart showing a powerful belt effect around Germany, Austria and, on the CEEC side, Poland, Czech Republic, Slovakia, Hungary and part of Slovenia. Moreover, we observe a double axis effect : on the one hand, towards the Eastern Balkans in the direction of Turkey, on the other, towards Russia via Poland. These two axes besides meet in Germany near Frankfurt. The dual mechanism of the vertical and horizontal division of labour within this whole can be clearly seen from the way trade has evolved between the Central European countries (CEFTA). Whereas the strict application of the vertical division of labour would have led to a star-like structure, this time towards Germany instead of Russia. The dynamics of trade within CEFTA indicate why the *Mitteleuropa* countries' area of geographical specialisation is relatively identical. This is typical of the belt effect. Two situations in particular are worth highlighting for they account for the present delimitation of the sub-regional belts, but also their possible expansion:

1) In the case of Slovenia, the simultaneous strong trade intensities with Germany and Italy show that in this particular *Mitteleuropa* zone we fall into another belt where either Italian firms or those that are established in Italy predominate;

2) In the case of Hungary, its strong trade intensity with Romania shows how belts can be deformed, in particular along axes that link the close-lying countries or regions because of their historico-cultural connectivity and complementarity over the years. While Hungary is evolving towards a system of intra-branch specialisation with Germany and Austria, Romania's comparative advantages enable it to not only take up the more traditional activities such as garments and furniture but also electronics and automobile assembly. In these sectors an increasing number of factories have come up along Hungary's border with

Romania, either because production, which has become too costly in Hungary, is being relocated here or to feed the Hungarian factories with components allowing them to gradually move up the technological ladder towards products with a higher value added. The same applies to the shortage of qualified engineers and technicians in Hungary, whom Romania is obviously able to supply at very competitive costs. This phenomenon illustrates the scenario known as the 'flight of wild gees' developed by the Japanese economist Kaname Akamatsu[54], famous for his study of the dynamic evolution of the division of labour in Asia, which Europe is in a position to partially reproduce today.

The South-East European Basin

A South-east European belt has emerged with Italy as its developed hub. On the geographical plane it greatly complements the *Mitteleuropa* belt and stretches from Slovenia to Greece, incorporating all the CEE countries of the zone, and in particular, the western Balkan states, which have not been included in our data because of the war in the former Yugoslavia. Along with Germany and France, Italy is involved in a game of strategy in the context of the ongoing European enlargement. Over and above the possibility of constituting simple trade markets in these transition economies, the productive localisation strategy, implemented since 1995, has enabled the traditional manufacturing sectors of the *Sistema Italia* (textiles, leather, furniture...) to reinstate their competitiveness, crippled by the huge rise in wage costs since the nineties, and penalised by infrastructural and labour market bottlenecks, which is precisely what the industrial North near this zone is suffering from. The state's resources have been mobilised with two objectives at least : the consolidation of the market share in countries where Italy enjoys a dominant position (number one supplier to Romania, second to Poland, third to Bulgaria, fourth to Hungary and sixth to the Czech

54. A theory, developed in the thirties and published in English in 1962, according to which Japan specialisation is 'flying' before the four NPIs or 'dragons' (Singapore, Taiwan, Hong Kong and South Korea), that are themselves followed by the four 'tigers' (Indonesia, Malaysia, Philippines and Thailand), and after that by China. For a description of the phenomenon see Jean-Joseph Boillot, 'The New Economic Geography of Asia', op. cit.

Republic) ; the boosting of FDIs by means of active participation in privatisation, acquisition of existing companies, and also joint-ventures. The Italian Ministry of Foreign Trade, in 1996, thus instituted a voluntarist policy whose key agencies are the *Instituto per il Commercio Estero* (ICE) and SIMEST (Financial corporation for the promotion of Italian firms abroad), which have considerable financial resources at their disposal. Primarily meant for assisting small and medium enterprises, the programmes proposed by these organisations have enabled Italian firms to build on their basic business activities, especially heavy industries (mechanics, industrial machinery, chemicals) but also the lighter sectors (shoes, textiles), at the same time distancing itself from the underlying logic of the big groups already present in central Europe : Montedison (energy, telecommunications), Eni (energy), Lucchini (steel), Parmalat and Barilla (agro-foods) and banks, including Unicredcito Italiano, increasingly active in the CEEC.

We should also note the role of Greece and Turkey in this space, which has been undergoing radical change since the demise of the Berlin Wall. Greece in particular has good coverage of the zone stretching from Bulgaria to Albania. Turkey has a lesser structural impact because of its limited commercial weight and its status of a candidate country in the same capacity as the others. But its role in the same radius of influence as Greece's and along the axis going up towards Germany via Romania, should not be under-estimated. The example of the distribution of tasks in the Renault group between its Bursa factory in Turkey, its Pitest factory in Romania and Revoz in Slovenia shows that these countries will have increasing structural links with each other.

Interestingly, the other European belts are rather marginal in this new geographical deal triggered by the eastern enlargement. But they were already quite impacted by the former enlargements towards the south in the 1970 and the North-East in the 1980s. With the last enlargement, their position should be affected both directly and indirectly.

The Old Post-war European Community Centre

The Netherlands geographical area well illustrates the position of the London-Paris-Frankfurt arc, considered the centre of EU15[55] and which the Commission prefers to describe as the North Yorkshire-Franche Compté-Hamburg triangle. In this zone resides one third of the EU15 population and it represents nearly half the revenues produced on one-seventh of the territory. As it happens, its direct relations with the CEEC are practically non-existent although, as we shall see later, a major portion of FDIs to these countries come from this triangle, especially in the services sector where it benefits from the strong points of the zonc on a pan-European scale, such as logistics and trade in the case of the Netherlands, finance in the UK and public services, cutting-edge industries, agro-foods and tourism in France.

In a certain number of sectors, where competition with the other three belts should intensify, especially in the manufacturing sector, a recent study by the consultancy firm Ernst & Young[56] enables us to better understand how this belt could draw on the growing complementarity in the high-tech field where a strong service component exists, to turn to good account the benefits flowing from the historic extension of the Single European Market. The distribution of 840 major investment projects inventoried by this firm in Greater Europe (25 countries), indicates that the attraction of the CEECs should be put into perspective, and especially *vis-à-vis* France, which ranks in second place (it receives 13 per cent of these projects), or the UK (16 per cent), which comes before Germany (9 per cent). In terms of regions, in 2002 and also in 2000, Ile-de-France (Paris region) thus formed part of the leading trio, besides London and Catalonia. In R&D, Ile-de-France is among the top European regions next to Catalonia, Madrid and Stockholm, whereas no region has emerged in Central Europe. Ile-de-France remains in fact number one in software. To this can be added centres like Grenoble, where STM, Motorola and Philips decided in the summer of 2002 to invest 2.8 billion euros in the research and manufacture of state-of-the-art semi-conductors. In relation to automobiles, Alsace is one of the most competitive regions along with Catalonia and Moscow. In chemicals, Rhône-Alpes (Lyon) retains its position of leader. As for the European automotive industry, not many know that the most

55. European Commission, Second Report on the Cohesion, op. cit.

56. Ernst & Young, European Investment Monitor, 2002.

productive factory of Europe in the broad sense is in Great Britain. It is the Nissan factory in Sunderland where 95 cars were produced per employee in 2001, as against 55 in the Skoda factories situated in Mlada Boleslav in the Czech Republic. Moreover, there was a difference of 40 per cent in the average price of the cars manufactured in the two factories ... to Nissan's advantage. A cross-analysis of sectors-regions shows that the gains of enlargement will depend on each one's capacity to adapt to the new deal and it is probably the diffused perception, and indeed the confused perception of this challenge that explains a certain anxiety on the part of the French regions in the context of the ongoing enlargement.

The Iberian Space

The Iberian area, composed of Spain and Portugal and partly connected to the French South West, is missing out on the eastward economic expansion. Resulting from the enlargement that took place in the mid-eighties, it is even seen as one of the big losers of this emergence of the CEECs on the European markets, because of its roughly equivalent specialisation, such as in textiles, agro-foods and even automobiles. Some macroeconomic studies[57] in their assessment of the distribution of the gains and losses of enlargement show that Spain and Portugal could be net losers, in particular because of the disappearance of important budgetary transfers from which the cohesion countries are still benefiting. However, these studies do not take into account the double frontage of the Iberian peninsula, i.e. towards the Mediterranean and towards Latin America, nor the capacity of reaction of the Atlantic arc, whose thirty regions have shown considerable dynamism. With port facades overlooking the Americas but also all the great maritime routes of the world, enlargement seems to simply constitute a challenge for these belts : namely to take full advantage of the development of coastal localisation, by definition better adapted to a globalised world economy. The Asian as well as American examples show that maritime frontage naturally has the most advantages for development. For all that, competition seems rather keen between the Iberian space and *Mitteleuropa*, as can be gauged from the transfer

57. See in chapter 1 the results of the simulations made by the Austrian institute WIFO.

in 2002 of the production of the Seat models to the Slovakian factories of the Volkswagen group.

The French Case

Where is France placed in this new configuration? Its position was definitely a very central one in Europe before the eastward enlargement. France had especially taken good advantage of the southward enlargement in the eighties. The situation changed significantly with the subsequent enlargement. If we keep to our description of the five belts, there seems to be a propensity of the French territory to expand in the direction of three centres : the old EU15 hub in the North and the Greater Paris region, the Iberian centre in the South-West and the Western zone of *Mitteleuropa* for eastern France. For the record, let us recall that only 520 kilometres separate Alsace from Poland, that is to say less than the distance to Brittany or to the Landes as the crow flies, and probably less in terms of transport time in view of the dense highway network crisscrossing Germany. The same goes for the Czech Republic, with which regions such as Colmar or even Dijon feel relatively closer than with the South West, for example. One case in particular is worth noting : Brittany. Its physical remoteness from the CEECs does not prevent it from heading the French regions in terms of the percentage of exports to the CEECs of its total exports (5.4 per cent). Essentially correlated to the weight of the agro-foods sales from Brittany to these countries, the case perfect illustrates the second principle that structures European space somewhat on the lines of the American *belt* model : the geographical remoteness factor can be compensated by very advanced pan-European specialisation. In a continuously expanding European space, and especially towards the East, it is an important option for the French regions to cultivate.

The trade figures of the various French regions in the last few years, however, show the hexagon's expansion in the new Europe. In particular there is a great degree of heterogeneity in the export orientation adopted by the French regions between the different European hubs and also in relation to the rest of the world. For example, the thrust of the French West is towards the American markets. Inversely, the importance of the Eastern markets for regions such as Alsace and Lorraine, has continued to grow. On the whole, the weight of the CEECs in the trade of the 22 French regions varies from 1 to 4 and the gap has widened in recent years. With the exception of Brittany, it is maximum for the Burgundy region (5 per cent of imports and exports) and minimum for the Midi-Pyrenees region (1.4 per cent).

From this point of view it is significant that the PSA group decided to invest huge sums in the central European automotive triangle, the very one where the Germans are so solid. But it is also the shortest distance from its Mulhouse and Sochaux factories, which will be working in conjunction with the central European factories. But this example does not constitute a general rule. Where firms are involved, we note that the French enterprises are very active in central Europe as a result of direct investment, i.e. a strategy applied to 'remote' countries precisely to compensate for their remoteness through direct siting with a pan-European agenda. They are thus the third most important investors in the CEECs after Germany and USA, and even the first in the two biggest countries, Poland and Romania. They have created their own space within the enlarged Europe and can take full benefit of the specialisation gains that are available at this time in the CEEC.

The Reinforcement of Sectoral Specialisation

Recent studies on the manner in which trade specialisation is evolving in the CEECs, and especially with the EU, put forward the hypothesis of a radical and rapid change of specialisation in the small countries involved in the catching-up process. The trade volumes under consideration will probably not change the specialisation map of Europe substantially and therefore of the location of industries. For all that, an analysis of the sectors where the CEECs have chosen to increase specialisation highlights a process that must be considered on two counts. Firstly, it globally reinforces the industries of the developed countries bordering the CEECs in the context of an increasingly intra-branch division of labour : there will be a much more detailed specialisation within the principal sectors themselves. Secondly, it enables an assessment of the quality of specialisation of the new EU countries and thus of the possible speed of convergence with European productivity levels. Here sectoral specialisation analysis uses the traditional Revealed Comparative Advantages

(RCA) index calculated by CEPII for the period 1993-99 and by Eurostat for 1999.[58] The data illustrates some significant changes that have taken place in just a few years.

Table 3.4

Evolution of the CEECs in the EU and French Total Import from the World

	1993	*1994*	*1995*	*1996*	*1997*	*1998*	*1999*
	Per cent CEECs' share in the EU total import						
Ready-made garments	9.62	11.07	11.67	12.09	11.97	13.48	13.06
Personnal car	1.03	1.02	1.47	1.73	2.01	3.37	3.89
Furnitures	7.65	8.93	10.75	11.1	11.31	11.93	12.33
Electronic consumer goods	0.25	0.61	1.47	2.1	5.5	7.77	8.86
Iron & Steel	3	4.61	5.12	4.57	4.92	4.92	4.21
Hosiery	3.69	4.27	4.65	5.23	4.75	5.84	5.97
Ships	5.21	4.67	5.14	4.47	1.67	2.24	7.92
	Per cent CEECs' share in the French total import						
Ready-made garments	0.58	0.65	0.86	0.77	0.82	0.77	0.89
Personnal car	1.36	1.69	2.66	2.64	3.31	3.49	4.1
Furnitures	0.51	1.04	1.51	1.15	1.07	1.61	0.94
Electronic consumer goods	0.18	0.08	0.16	0.08	1.18	1	0.85
Iron & Steel	0.15	0.15	0.17	0.17	0.11	0.14	0.18
Hosiery	0.43	0.46	0.46	0.44	0.47	0.55	0.79
Ships	2.44	1.73	2.42	3.18	2.46	1.97	1.47

Source: CEPII, Chelem, 2001.

In the traditional sectors necessitating less or averagely qualified intensive labour (textiles-garments, furniture, agro-foods), the CEEC have maintained and even improved their strong points. At the same time we observe that their relative weight in the global EU exports has continued to gain in importance, thereby indicating a dual phenomenon:

58. Tim Allen, Eurostat, Statistiques in brief, topic 6 – 6/2001 ; Mohammed Hedi Behir, Mathilde Maurel, 'Impacts économiques et sociaux de l'élargissement pour l'Union européenne et la France', CEPII, a report for the French Senate, December 2001. The comparative advantage index used by T. Allen is of the type : ((Xp-Mp) – [(X-M) * ((Xp+Mp)/(X+M))] * 1000/GDP, calculations done at the 4 digit level of the STCI classification. The indicator used by the CEPII is of the type Balance Contribution: (1000/X+M) * { (Xj Mj) – (Xj+MJ)/(X+M) }. It is thus not weighted by the GDP, unlike the indicator developed by Eurostat.

1) The total exports of these economies in these fields has increased in value and thus indicates their growing specialisation ;

2) The EU, for its part, has continued to import relatively more from the neighbouring economies to the detriment of other emerging zones traditionally supplying these types of products. This particularly concerns some parts of Asia where costs have continued to rise in this last decade, while they have taken to specialising in other fields, such as electronics. The competitive ousting of the Mediterranean countries, as for example in the textile-clothing sector, is a little more awkward for Europe in the sense that these countries do not have many other industrial advantages to fall back on.

In the traditional raw material intensive sectors, such as Steel and Chemicals, the CEEC specialisation arises from infrastructure that existed during the COMECON period and illustrates the ratchet or the lock-in effect[59] of previous specialisation. But the lack of abundant resources in most of these countries, as well as the technologically obsolete processes explains the gradual erosion of the entire region. Despite specific advantages found in some countries, the FDI map shows that these sectors are not particularly attractive, and requests for restructuring from the EU (in iron and steel for example) as well as the new environmental restrictions resulting from accession, should accelerate the abandonment of these sectors in the coming years. The trend is clearly discernable in the evolution of the CEECs' share in the global import of iron and steel from the EU, which has been stagnating at 4 points throughout the decade, while it has gone from 9.6 to 13 points for ready-to-wear garments and from 7.6 to 12.3 points for furniture.

A major outcome for the CEECs from the global point of view is the emergence of new comparative advantages or strong points in the automotive and home electronics sectors. These are two sectors in which these countries had definite comparative disadvantages before transition, despite efforts at industrialisation and modernisation in these fields, in particular through numerous cooperation agreements with Western partners. The volumes involved are significant from the European point of view as in 1999 these countries represented

59. In the sense that the closure for example of a steel factory with a production capacity of 10 million tonnes requires several years to complete.

4 and 9 per cent respectively of the global EU imports of individual cars and home electronics. A comparison of the individual cars sector with the vehicle branch as a whole (which also includes spare parts) is however still showing an overall shortfall. This is explained by the import of up-market cars in comparison to the vehicles exported but, perhaps rather surprisingly, by the import of components manufactured in Western Europe under conditions of increasing returns and higher technologies that justify keeping their production in the EU15. France is thus one of the principal manufacturers of automobile components of which a great number are exported to the Iberian peninsula and now to the CEECs.

At the same time, the nature of specialisation has gradually changed. If the traditional sectors always correspond to a classic intra-branch specialisation, the more recently acquired specialisation shows a rapid evolution towards intra-branch trade. In other words, it is already much more integrated with the processes of European production, and therefore technologically speaking it is much closer. The CEPII experts have above all noted a rapid rise in intra-branch trade, increasingly horizontal in nature, i.e. within the same product line. The Czech Republic is particularly in advance in this respect. Here we can give the example of 'Fabia', a small car manufactured by Skoda and commercially classed in the same category as the small 'Ibiza' produced by Seat. Both are similar to Volkswagen's 'Polo' model and even to the 'Golf', one of the earlier models in the series. The German manufacturer, who controls all these brands and sells them simultaneously on all markets, has to project a more sportive and young image for Ibiza in order to differentiate it from the other models. Skoda, on the other hand, has a more 'family' profile, which the French publicists focused on at the time of its launch in France in 2002.

Vincent Vicard also showed in a recent study[60] that cross-trade of similar goods has gone up considerably to the detriment of specialised trade. In fact, the CEECs have a propensity to catch up with the mode of specialisation of the EU15 corresponding to their level of convergence. In this respect, the Czech Republic had in 1998

60. Vincent Vicard, Endogénéité des critères de zone monétaire optimale et commerce intra-branche', M. Phil dissertation, University Paris I, 2001 and visit the CEPII web site for the english version : www.cepii.org

already overtaken the European average, Hungary was not far behind, but Greece surprisingly enough was very behind and was placed below Romania, a country whose specialisation was the most traditional.

Specialisation is moreover dynamic. This can be seen from the fact that the traditional sectors tend to be relegated to the more backward countries. For example, the textile-garment industry is gradually relocating itself in Romania and Bulgaria and within Poland, to its East, and even towards Belarus and the Ukraine. At the same time, intra-branch specialisation is becoming stronger in the more advanced countries such as Hungary, Czech Republic and Slovenia.

But the Dynamics of Country-wise Specialisation is Unequal

The global analysis of the region however masks some key facts necessary for an understanding of the mode and dynamics of integration of the CEE countries. A country-wise analysis thus shows both horizontal and vertical differences and more or less rapid dynamics of improvement in the specialisation. It is thus possible to identify each country with two or three key products, for example, Estonia with mobile telephones, Poland and Romania with furniture and Hungary with electronics.

Eurostat's lengthy calculations firstly confirm a very great degree of sectoral specialisation, coherent with the size and increasing liberalisation of the economy. It illustrates the unprecedented magnitude of the restructuring that took place in the erstwhile COMECON countries. This was done through a process of creative destruction unmatched in the peacetime history of economics, which to a great extent explains the slow pace of macroeconomic development in the initial years. On the whole, from 1998 onwards each country only advanced by 3 to 4 strong points in terms of contribution to the balance of trade.

Partly a corollary of intensive specialisation, the entire region could have specialised in the same group of products, as it happened in Asia with textiles and electronics. In fact, each country is often associated with a rather original specialisation both in terms of products as well as in terms of the nature of the division of labour, and even the specialisation processes. We can, for example compare Hungary with the Czech Republic. Hungary is very open to different segments both upstream and downstream of the same product chain. With regard to automobiles Hungary manufactures car motors in bulk and imports the complete vehicle and in the case of electronics it assembles components imported from Asia. The Czech Republic on the other hand is able to master the entire automobile chain quite easily. Whereas moving up the chain is vertical in the Czech case, it is horizontal in the Hungarian case: from computers plastic to motor vehicle equipments manufacturers, then production of electronic components (and call centers later) and reinforcement of pharmaceutical specialisation.

A key phenomenon, specialisation seems to evolve within the regional subsets according to two lines of force, which produce rather contradictory results in terms of the concentration or dispersion of activities in the larger Europe:

1) Firstly, the dual strategy of cross-border countries : offensive reinforcement of their strong points thanks to the competitiveness of the neighbouring CEECs in products or range of products in which these countries had lost their edge. The Nordic countries, Germany and Austria and eventually Italy, simultaneously proceeded to locate their traditional industries, such as leather and textiles, in their respective CEEC zones. It was the same in the case of furniture. The agenda followed by Germany in the case of automobiles was nearly identical as we can see from the Volvo group's decision to set up factories in the Baltic States. Similarly, in the telecommunications sector, Finnish and Swedish firms set up mobile telephone assembly units in the Baltic countries. This trend will lead to the increasing specialisation of European space through the formation of large belts. Especially as the big multinationals of the more distant countries are tempted to take advantage of the competitive edge offered by the principal European centres. With regard to automobiles, the American groups present in Germany have copied the German manufacturers and also taken advantage of the same sub-contracting networks and the agglomeration effects occurring in the entire region. By the same token, PSA plans to invest in the Czech Republic and use the factory originally built for BMW.

2) Secondly, strategies adopted by transnational firms of the non-cross border countries. The latter try to take advantage of the CEECs' location on the periphery of the developed European markets, and set up new specialised activities there. Next, they try to conquer markets despite competition from the cross-border countries. The first blueprint for this is the electronics sector in Hungary, which does not really correspond to Germany or Austria's strong points. In this scenario the CEECs widen their range of specialisation and reduce the degree of specialisation of the large European belts to which they belong. The second blueprint can be illustrated by the Renault group's strategy which, after it failed to acquire the Skoda group, bought out the Romanian manufacturer, Dacia, to make it into a regional development base for its introductory model, whose characteristics corresponded with the demand in these countries. Its older set up in Slovenia had the same aim, i.e. to be directly present in a zone under German or Italian influence. Thus this country has in a few years become one of the major automobile centres in the Balkans.

On the whole, the specialisation and localisation map in the candidate countries is evolving rapidly but in a rather ambivalent manner. The space of firms and that of nations do not really correspond. Despite the narrowing down of specialisation in each country of the region around specific strong points, this space is broadly developing a dense and varied industrial fabric. It is a blueprint that corresponds quite well to the opinion vouchsafed by the above-mentioned American economist, P. Krugman. The European space does not seem to follow the very distinct principles of specialisation existing in the United States. One of the major reasons according to him is the role of history on territories and the fact that the European population is not very mobile (partly linked). Thus, enlargement should not have much of an impact on one of Europe's unique characteristics: its different regions will trade many similar products and specialisation will become very fine-tuned. The undeniable competition provided by the CEECs thus supposes that each country will place itself as best it can in the European matrix of costs and product mix[61], in view of the arrival on the scene of

61. Industrial configuration in which we find, on the one hand, production costs varying on a scale of 1 to 10, depending on the country in the larger Europe, on the other, specialisation in the product line or niche for which an enterprise in a given territory remains fully competitive in this continental space.

these new countries. It is a question of niche for individual manufacturers and the enhancement of the agglomeration effect for territorial administration, which are partly responsible for stimulating the competitiveness of territories in Greater Europe.

4

Sectoral Dynamics

Taking into consideration the shock of transition and the relatively small size of the Central and East European economies, the enlargement of the European economic space did not have a major impact on localisation of production at the continental level and is not expected to in the short term. The tone of some articles on the eastward shifting of industries was no doubt somewhat alarmist. However, they abstained from mentioning that only small sums were involved and that the sectors in question involved activities that would be impelled to restructure because of technological advances or enhanced labour specialisation at the international level. Typical examples are the leather-garment and the automotive industries. Moreover, for many products the CEECs paradoxically facilitated the repatriation to Europe of activities that had relocated or were in the process of relocating in Asia.

However, the challenges in the medium term consequent to the economic convergence of these countries in the context of a new European space with its many new markets and as many new producers, should not be under-estimated. Fifty million workers from the twelve candidate countries (80 million if the Balkans and Turkey are included) will now swell the 185 million strong workforce of the EU15. Nevertheless, contrary to the unilateral fears of the risk of 'massive' relocation of industries from the West to the East, the geographical re-organisation of activities at the continental level should follow a positive sum game, i.e. be beneficial to both the member states as well as the applicant countries. According to the economic theory on large markets, this means that the re-organisation of localisation on the basis of the principles of modern economic geography must be rightly anticipated. Competition between regions, i.e the choice of sites does in no way depend exclusively on salary levels. The productivity of firms, especially groups of firms, and therefore of activity zones, their technological level, the effect of increasing returns and the variety of product lines, the skill/qualification level of the workforce, the mastery of logistics are the real determinants of competitiveness in the new European space. Against this backdrop, the motivations of investors in the CEECs perfectly reflect the new deal.

Firstly, the aim of more than two-thirds of FDIs in the candidate countries is to meet the internal requirements of a region whose standard of living is rapidly catching up with that of Western Europe. This is clearly visible in the case of automobiles, the production capacity of which will be nearly 2.5 million vehicles by 2007, i.e. equal to current French production. This increase in production and consumption levels will also have an impact on the anticipated annual automobile sales in the CEECs in 2008-2010. However, the problem is the competitive distribution of the different models of cars that will be manufactured either in the West or the East, as well as the components necessary for their manufacture. It is imperative for firms in the more developed zones to anticipate and accordingly plan the up-market range. This is illustrated by the major decision taken by Volkswagen in September 2002 to relinquish the small *Lupo* and *Polo* models to Skoda and in the short term, to transfer the production of the Spanish *Ibiza,* manufactured by Seat for the Eastern markets, to its Slovakian factory.

Secondly, out of the one-fourth FDIs motivated by localisation in order to make exports more competitive, a volume which is certainly not negligible if we consider the annual flow of FDI to the CEECs (20 billion euros per annum), in reality how much will be used to generate production in eastern Europe to stop continental consumers buying from the more distant locations, especially Asian? The Italian example in the garment sector shows that Romania and Bulgaria at present constitute perfect substitutes for medium range articles of limited production runs, which are generally labour intensive but do not necessitate a highly skilled workforce. How many units would have eventually closed down because of the simple dynamics of technological progress and productivity gains? This refers especially to automobile equipment, where the productivity gain imposed by car manufacturers is around 8-10 per cent per annum because of the natural decline in the relative demand for automobiles (income elasticity and product cycle effect), and which can only be sustained through constant innovation and lowering of the relative price. Therefore, enlargement should not become a scapegoat for structural change, but it should be understood that the new pan-European division of labour will enable coverage of a greater number of production segments in the context of increased manufacturing activity world-wide.

The fact remains that in the extended European space, the territories will have to adapt and specialise further in the new matrix of costs and types of demand in order to integrate harmoniously with dynamic growth at the continental level. In contrast to the previous chapter the following pages adopt a micro-economic and sectoral approach. The objective is to highlight the prospective industrial stakes in a realistic manner, i.e. without excessive optimism with regard to the challenges before the concerned industries, but also without excessive pessimism. As the annual report by Ernst & Young on large-scale investment projects at the pan-European level in 2001-2002 shows, most French regions remain the choice location both for high tech activities (Ile-de-France for R&D, Rhône-Alpes for electronics and chemicals, etc.), and for the up-market segments of the more classic industries : for example Northern France and Alsace for automobiles.[62] But the new challenges of the continentalisation of Greater Europe should not be under-estimated. The distribution of the potential gains of enlargement will depend on the adaptation capacity of each region to the new deal of comparative advantages.

Textile-Garments: Inroads into a Global Industry, but for How Long?

There has been a steady decline in the growth of global trade in the textile-garments field since the early nineties. Thus, it was only 4 per cent per annum between 1990 and 2000. Global exports of the entire branch rose to 280 billion dollars in 2000, or 5 per cent of global manufacturing trade, but this sector remained in third place after electronics and automobiles.

62. Ernst & Young, *European Investment Monitor*, 2002.

The Regionalisation of Global Trade in Favour of the CEECs

The analysis of trade of the last 20 years shows that the CEEC transition combined with the trend towards geographic concentration of the textile trade around the major centres of the global economy. On the one hand, although the industrialised countries have increased imports of textile-garments, their relative share in the global imports has diminished as a result of the emergence of new markets linked to the acute demographic distortion of the planet in favour of the developing countries. On the other, these same developing countries are exporting more and more (33-53 per cent of global textile-garment exports) and their share in the imports of the industrialised countries is more than 55 per cent. The trend should intensify with the suspension of the Multifibre Agreement[63] by 2005. The developing countries are increasingly exporting garments characterized by more labour intensive production processes ; as yarn and fabric necessitate more capital intensive installations (20 per cent of the total), they are the prerogative of the industrialised countries such as Japan, Germany or even France.

Among the developing countries, competition is very keen between the various sub-regions. The global share of exports from Asia (including India) peaked in 1994, then declined and stabilised at 33 per cent. However, exports from continental China multiplied 17 times between 1980 and 2000, their relative weight increasing from 4.2 per cent to 11 per cent of global trade. It should be noted that China's gains in developing zones such as Latin America, Africa or the Middle-East are just as remarkable in all the international markets as a whole. They denote the emergence of a global supply of medium to low-end range products that essentially meet the needs of the developing countries.

---

63. Agreement signed in 1973 during the oil crisis. It aimed to protect the importing countries against competition from the emerging countries, especially from those with a sizable textile industry (East Asia). It authorised decreasing quantitative restrictions and self-limitating bilateral agreements. Its discontinuance is scheduled for January 1, 2005.

Figure 4.1

CEECs Share in the World and EU Import of Textiles (garment included)

World Import

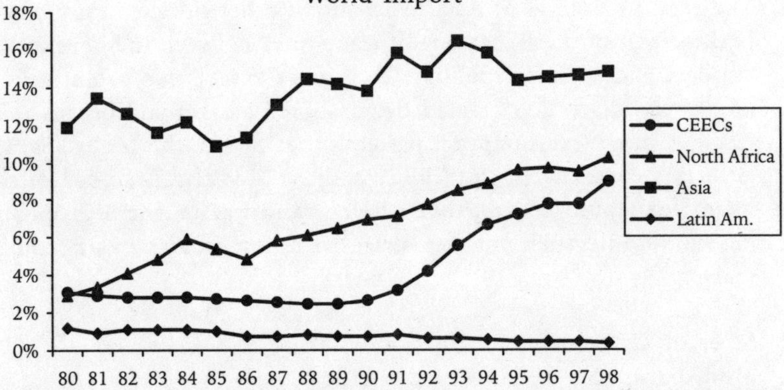

World Import	80	81	82	83	84	85	86	87	88	89	90	91	92	93	94	95	96	97	98
CEECs	3	3	3	3	3	3	3	3	2	2	3	3	4	6	7	7	8	8	9
North Africa	3	3	4	5	6	5	5	6	6	7	7	7	8	8	9	10	10	10	10
Asia	12	13	13	12	12	11	11	13	14	14	14	16	15	16	16	14	15	15	15
Latin Am.	1	1	1	1	1	1	1	1	1	1	1	1	1	1	1	0	0	0	0

EU15 Import

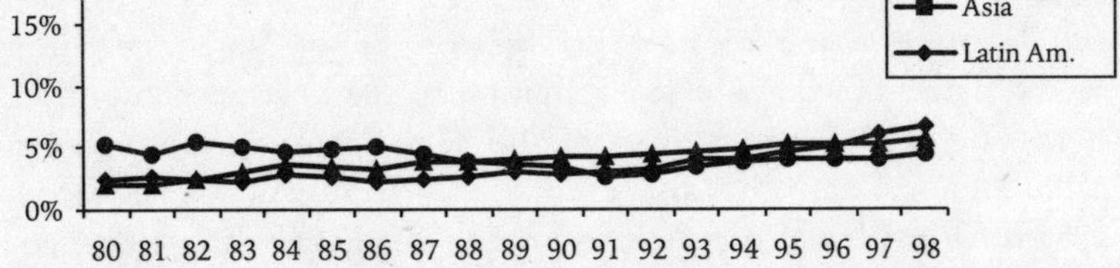

EU15 Import	80	81	82	83	84	85	86	87	88	89	90	91	92	93	94	95	96	97	98
CEECs	5	5	5	5	5	5	5	5	4	4	3	3	3	3	4	4	4	4	5
North Africa	2	2	3	3	4	3	3	4	4	4	4	4	4	5	5	5	5	5	6
Asia	20	24	24	25	27	26	26	28	31	32	29	32	32	35	36	34	33	33	32
Latin Am.	2	3	2	2	3	3	2	2	3	3	3	3	3	4	4	5	5	6	7

Source: Chelem CEPII

Notwithstanding this specifically Chinese phenomenon, the progression of developing countries in the global textile trade is accompanied by a type of concentration of their exports around three major consumption poles : Europe, United States and Asia. The relative decline of Asia in favour of other developing regions is the result of the tightening of trade links between the developed markets and their peripheries. To a great extent this evolution is due to the distortion created by the quota system and because of changes in the consumption patterns that favour shorter cycles. It is in this context that the CEECs and the Mediterranean countries have been able to improve their standing on the European markets while their market share in other sectors has become marginal.

Shorter Cycle: Mediterranean-CEEC Versus Asia

However, the development of Asian exports, which began in the late fifties, differs from the processes at work in the Mediterranean and CEE countries since 1990. From the sixties, the United States and Europe, followed by Japan, began to shop in Asia. The rise in this demand enabled the newly industrialised countries (NIC) of Asia to rely on the clothing industry to move up the textile value chain and enter into the production and export of yarn and textiles and thereafter, artificial fibres. From the eighties, these countries had to face competition from China. Asian manufacturers (Hong Kong, Taiwan) were the first to sub-contract in China and the European and American buyers followed by shifting their supply zone towards the Chinese continent.

The emergence of new production zones in the eighties followed the slowdown of consumption in the developed countries. It coincided with the growth of the demand for variety and low priced goods and the appearance of specialised chain stores proposing articles at competitive prices. To adjust to these changes, industrialists had to shorten the production cycles. This imperative forced them to reduce the distance between the production and the consumption zones, thus contributing to the localisation of the

German, then French industries in Spain and Portugal and thereafter in Turkey, Tunisia and Morocco. From 1990, this movement gained momentum at the global level with, on the one hand, the Caribbean plan and the creation of Alena[64], which accelerated the localisation of American (and Asian) industry in countries neighbouring it; and on the other, the liberalisation of the former Communist bloc, which exerted a pull effect on European industry.

Within the EU, Germany, which had long practised the outward processing of traffic[65] (OPT) by sub-contracting in the socialist countries (starting with the German Democratic Republic), continued the practice on a larger scale after 1989. In Italy, Europe's biggest garment manufacturer, the advantages provided by industrial districts (the Prato province in North Italy was an exceptional model of competitiveness) combined with the protection offered by a piecemeal retail operation, for a long time enabled the industry to resist Asian competition. However, in the nineties, consequent to the appreciation of the lira, the Italian industry was in turn compelled to move their production elsewhere. It chose the CEECs, and in particular Romania. Thus in the course of these years, Asia's share of European garments imports (17 per cent in 1998) fell, while that of the Mediterranean region went up, eventually overtaken by the export boom in the Central and East European countries.

---

64. North American Free Trade Agreement or NAFTA. Trade agreement first between the United States and Canada (which came into force on January 1, 1989) then with Mexico (January 1, 1994) granting the importers of the zone a very favourable customs regimen if their products met the stipulated conditions of admissibility. The Caribbean plan, on its side, offered trade benefits to the countries of this region so that their products could access the North American markets.

65. The outward processing traffic (OPT) is a customs regime introduced in the European Community in 1986, which allows the temporary export of goods for transformation, finishing or repairs, which are then re-imported, but are totally or partially exempt from customs duty.

Table 4.1

CEECs in the French Textiles Trade between 1990 and 2000

	French Import of Garments		*French Export of Textiles*	
	1990	*2000*	*1990*	*2000*
CEECs	3.7	6.8	3.2	9.0
North Africa	17.7	18.9	10.3	15.9
Asia	19.0	35.3	2.7	4.0
Latin America	1.5	0.4	0.5	0.8
sub-total	41.9	61.5	16.8	29.7
Total (Mds €)	8.8	14.3	5.8	7.6

Source: Chelem CEPII 2002.

France's case is instructive in this regard. In 1999, France was the 7th biggest textile exporter in the world and the 6th for garments, but it was also the 6th biggest importer of textiles and clothing. The evolution of its trade resembles that of the EU. The share of garment imports from emerging countries increased from 42 per cent to 62 per cent between 1990 and 2000, as we can see in Table 19. On the other hand French fabric sales to the rest of the world progressed equally well even if the direct share of the emerging countries remained less than 30 per cent in 2000. The remainder was exported to the other developed countries, of which a considerable portion is used in the sub-contracting activity of Italian, German, etc. firms, in these same emerging countries. Differences between these various zones and especially the CEECs in comparison with Asia, should be highlighted. The weight of the CEECs in garment imports to France increased notably during the past decade. At the same time the share of the Mediterranean countries stagnated and in the case of the Asian countries, it doubled. The CEECs in reality helped to bring down Western Europe's imports from Asia in the context of the latter's greater competitiveness in comparison with the Mediterranean countries. The picture presented by textile exports from our markets is even more instructive. Asia imports practically no textiles from France, so that the overall balance of this sector has continued to deteriorate. On the contrary, the CEECs as well as the Mediterranean countries constitute huge markets for French fabric, so that the textile-garment cycle with these two zones functions quite well. The same mechanism is found in the other European countries, the one difference being that France is relatively more aligned with the South than with the East, contrary to the German or Nordic buyers.

Clothing: The Take-off of Short Supply Cycles in Europe

Since 1990, the CEECs have thus become the textile hub of Europe. In 2000, they represented an average 21 per cent of extra-EU clothing imports, but with Italy importing as much as 36 per cent and Germany 31 per cent. The CEECs were just behind the Mediterranean countries in exports (23 per cent), but the two regions together weighed as much as Asia. The positioning of the CEECs is a bit special : it is more oriented towards the medium and up-market range and smaller production series, while the low end mass-produced series remains the prerogative of the Asian countries. The integration of the zone into the European industrial circuits of the sector was rapid as sub-contracting accounted for nearly 80 per cent of its exports. Strategic sub-contracting, aimed at earning foreign exchange quickly, represented more than 50 per cent of the production capacity of the Czech Republic, 58 per cent of Hungary's and up to 90-95 per cent of Croatia's. In the latter country, in fact, the Benetton group had employed more than 2000 workers in 2000.

Instead of sub-contracting, there was also the possibility of the principals choosing to set up a plant directly, thus limiting the number of intermediaries. This is what Archimode and Levi-Strauss did in Poland, Pierre Cardin and Steilmann in Romania, and Chantelle and Lafuma in Hungary. The faster pace of the market turnover of new collections produced in small series needs quick responses, which are easier to coordinate if the unit is within close geographic proximity than when it is thousands of kilometres away in a totally different culture. The choice between setting up a plant and remote-controlled sub-contracting depends on several factors and individual strategies but, whatever the choice, the emergence of the CEECs as the target of European manufacturers is undeniable.

Situated in Western Europe's backyard, the candidate countries are able to perfectly satisfy the demands of shorter cycles. The major chain stores, such as Mango, Zara or Promod have revolutionised the practices of this sector by accelerating the launch of new collections. By producing a limited series of a particular design they also limit stocks, and therefore have to react more quickly to the demand for a specific design. In view of this phenomenon, the reduction in the distance between production and consumption zones becomes crucial. For example, Italy and Germany sub-contract most of their requirements either in Romania or the Czech Republic. In 1999, one-third of the outward processing traffic to Romania and 60 per cent of Czech export orders came from German principals. With borders vanishing and infrastructural development taking place, the time taken will be further reduced. The absence of maritime transport, less expensive but slower than road transport, in this context gives the CEECs an advantage over the Mediterranean countries. But for how long, in view of the inevitable convergence of wages?

Can Wages Convergence Put a Brake on Textile Development in the CEECs

Knowing that salaries represent as much as 35 per cent of the production costs in garment manufacturing and that sewing machine operations account for 75 per cent of manufacturing time even today (10 per cent in the case of textiles, which are much more capital intensive), this component remains an important factor in the choice of localisation. For example, in the manufacture of a shirt, payments to workers represent 53 per cent of the total cost in France and 28 per cent in China. Can the rise in gross pay scales in the zone put the textile sector into jeopardy? Probably not in the short term and this is for three reasons: qualification level; cheaper labour reserves in the more remote regions; lastly, an eastward and southward geographical shift.

Lower wage costs were initially a major factor of attraction, but everyone knows that it is not a permanent phenomenon, especially in the more advanced countries. Instead qualifications and a reputation for quality work enabled the CEECs to make intricate garments and accessories (suits, swim-suits, bags....) and to justify, at least partially, higher costs per minute as compared to some Asian countries. Each country has its own traditional skills : long-sleeved clothes and outerwear garments in jersey for women in Hungary; under-garments in the Czech Republic; classic ready-to-wear for men and women, hosiery, woven fabrics and under-garments in Poland. However, a European manufacturer would not sub-contract his collection of delicate textiles such as silk in these countries.

Although the wage increase in textiles in 2000, was more than 20 per cent in Hungary and about 5 per cent in the Czech Republic, the persistence of strong regional contrasts still enables these countries to benefit from competitive localisation, which continues to exert a pull-effect and will do so for some years to come. In this sector, the wage difference is around 30 per cent between the East and West of Hungary. The same applies to Poland between Poznàn and Warsaw and to the north or the south east of the country which possess important labour reserves because of the particularly high level of unemployment.

The pressure exerted by high wage costs, especially when expressed in euros, nevertheless justifies a shift in textile manufacture towards other countries of the less developed regions, such as Romania, Bulgaria, and even Ukraine and Belorussia. Romania thus became the EU's biggest supplier in this sector in 1999, a position which was confirmed in 2000, with Poland, which had occupied the first place until 1998, now in second. In the context of the outward processing traffic (OPT), Romanian garment exports to Europe attained 1.2 billion euros in 1999, 21 per cent more than in 1998, while the other Romanian textile exports amounted to nearly 0.8 billion euros (+66 per cent). A combination of factors explains Romania's success in this field. In comparison to its neighbours, the Romanian garment sector has the advantage of a qualified but much cheaper workforce. Despite the considerable delay in infrastructure development, it is sufficiently close geographically to respond to the principals' 'just-in-time policy', which tries to avoid building stocks. Lastly, it has opened up its economy with taxes and quotas with the EU abolished in 1997. In Romania the cost of one minute of production is one of the lowest in the world : 0.12 euro/minute, not including transport (between 1 and 3 per cent of the cost price), that is less than Poland (0.15 euros), or Sri Lanka or Mexico. Positioned between Tawain (0.2 euros) and China (0.09 euros), it can even be competitive in relation to Asia. Albania and the Ukraine offer even lower costs, but their political instability is a handicap.

As for Bulgaria, Bulgaria's textile trade recorded in the nineties the most dynamic growth of all its industrial sectors. As elsewhere, there has been a simultaneous rise of both imports and exports. In

2000, the textile sector came second in the overall exports (17 per cent with 831 million dollars[66]) just after ferrous and non-ferrous metals. The balance of trade in this sector progressed from 3.5 million in 1992 to 10.4 million dollars in 2000 – a small increase perhaps but which reflects rather well the cross-trade process with the developed European countries. On the product front, heading the list are the different types of clothing for both men and women (suits, jackets, pants, dresses, skirts, shirts) followed by jersey items. Special order work represents 80 to 90 per cent of the total Bulgarian textile production. As in the other CEECs, the principal asset is the skilled and cheap labour. According to the professionals of the sector, production costs (not including transport) in 2000 came to approximately 0.05 euro/minute on an average, but there are also manufacturers who propose 0.03 euro/minute. The monthly salaries in the Bulgarian textile sector are among the lowest in the industry : 82 euros in 2000. Despite competitive prices, the sector's share in Bulgarian industrial production continues to decline : 5.5 per cent in 1999 to 5.3 per cent in 2000. There is also a constant reduction of the workforce (122,350 workers employed in 2000 as against 132,967 in 1998). The productivity gains as a result of global competition outstrip the growth of the quantity exported.

The Emergence of a Complete Textile Chain will Probably Run Up against the Shortcomings of Local Industrialists

Most of the region's firms work within the framework of the outward or inward processing traffic[67] (90 per cent of Romanian and Hungarian production). In this system the importer has to give a bank guarantee to the customs department, the guaranteed amount depending on the value of the goods and the customs duty levied on it, in order to check temporary imports that could turn out to be final (diversion of goods for the local market). When the good is re-exported, the deposit is fully restituted, provided that, in the case of transformed goods, proof is submitted that the quantity being re-expedited (the pieces and rejected items have also to be declared)

66. Figures in US dollar given by the Belgian authorities.

67. Contrary to the OPT, the inward processing traffic (IPT) concerns imported goods that are thereafter transformed then re-exported, benefiting from a favourable customs regimen.

corresponds to that which was brought in. Foreign firms are exempt from VAT and customs duties on the imported raw materials used for reexports. This system encouraged foreign enterprises to sub-contract in this region, even when customs duties were high. But it has also created a dependency, which could prove harmful for the future: it is paradoxically difficult for local enterprises operating within this framework to free themselves and to prosper. The first option would presuppose an investment capacity that the strict system of OPT (Outward Processing Traffic) does not favour. In a scenario of small and medium enterprises and run-down equipment, the quantities produced by local sub-contractors are small. No Central European company is classed among the 300 biggest in the sector[68]. The major national enterprises were all split up under the privatisation policy. In 1997, 55 per cent firms employed less than 10 workers in Hungary, and in the Czech Republic, enterprises with less than 200 workers were responsible for more than half the production in 1999.

As for the second option, the low margins granted in the context of the OPT only ensure that operating costs and wages are met, thus limiting the capacity to invest in the productive apparatus and to create their own brands. The firms themselves are not very keen to invest. The local markets do not offer any big outlets, at least in the ranges that firms normally work with. This makes them fragile and hence local firms risk being confined to regions where wage costs are low.

The prospect of moving up the chain and undertaking textile manufacture, a much more capital-intensive activity (as some NICs in Asia have done) is limited. Hence, their development could translate into the growth of services both upstream and downstream of the sector. That is, they would not only be concerned with production but also with the supply and logistics of raw materials. This would signify that the share of the end retailers among the principals would continue to grow. At present, although there are instances when manufacturers are allowed to procure supplies of yarn and accessories from the local market, 90 per cent of the materials are provided and managed by the principals. This development also presupposes access to bank credit, a facility that is still not very

68. Textilewirtchfat, February 2001.

developed in the CEECs. For the first wave of CEECs, this provided a respite in the medium term in view of competition from the second wave of CEECs and, more so perhaps, from the Mediterranean countries, in particular Turkey.

Furniture: Old Suppliers and a Local Demand that is Gradually Gaining in Strength

The Success of Post-Communist Conversion

Largely self-sufficient during the Communist era, but once again completely outmoded in terms of technology and design, since 1990 the furniture industry has become one of the most dynamic sectors of the CEECs thanks to the strategy of rapid liberalisation. This evolution found expression in the modification and increase in production in the entire region. In Hungary, the industry has displayed amazing dynamism with the production valued at 316 million euros in 2000 as against 240 million in 1999. In Poland, production has quadrupled since the early nineties and today represents a little more than 4 per cent of the jobs. Romania, which had opened up considerably during Ceausescu's term in office, is trying to supplant countries that have become expensive in terms of wage costs.

These results can firstly be attributed to a dynamic export sector, while sales on the local market, which went through a period of depression until these last few years, as did all consumption, come in a poor second. In effect, the recent privatisation and investments in the CEECs, especially by foreign groups, have enabled the furniture industry to equip itself with high-tech equipments. The European enterprises, attracted by the low costs of production, a skilled workforce and the presence of raw materials (especially wood), have invested massively in the region, in particular the Germans in Poland and the Italians in Romania. In Poland, in June 2001, foreign firms (mainly Dutch, German and Swedish) had invested more than 150 million euros. But the sub-contracting business has been affected even more. The furniture giant, Ikea, has at its disposal a network of several hundred local suppliers.

These linkages have encouraged the transfer of technologies and also promoted the enterprises of the zone abroad. This statement, however, needs to be qualified. It is true that the European groups

Figure 4.2

Evolution of the Furniture Trade from CEE 1995-2000*

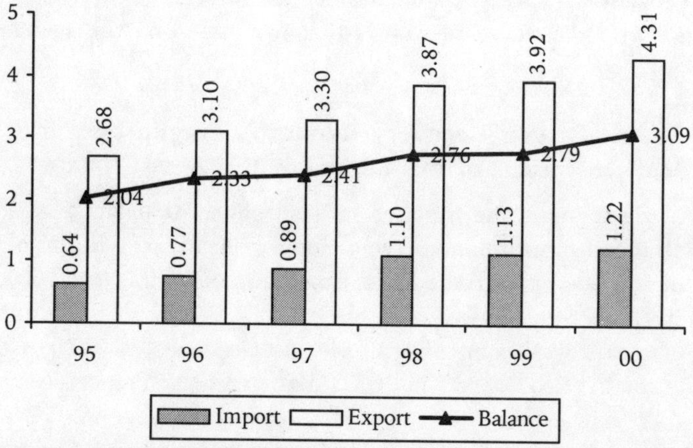

* Six major Eastern European countries: Poland, Czech R.,Slovakia, Hungary, Romania and Bulgaria.

Source: UN statistical data base Comtrade 2002.

by buying shares in the local Polish companies and investing massively in the production capacity and know-how have opened their markets to the local Polish companies. The latter are now capable of producing furniture that meets the requirements of West European consumers. On the other hand, Romania is still seen as a country where sub-contracting activity is primordial. Under pressure from the principals, especially the central purchasing agencies, the Romanian subsidiaries import their raw materials, transform them and then re-export them to the end markets. The furniture industry by itself is responsible for 17 per cent of the exports of these countries. The fiscal advantages granted to exporters since the beginning of 2000 (taxation on profits from exports reduced to 5 per cent), and the cheap yet experienced workforce, have played a major role in propelling growth of Romanian exports. It remains to be seen whether this industry can climb higher in the manufacturing and distribution chain, as it has been able to do in Poland, and thus partly free itself from the exacting sub-contracting relationship. Or whether, as in the case of textile-garments, it will remain ensconced in a relationship of strong dependence *vis-à-vis* its principals, and therefore subject to the risk of localisation further to the east where there is a chance of wage costs remaining low for a longer time. But the present dynamism of the Italian manufacturers and also the French, on Romanian soil, shows that this is not on the agenda as yet.

An Export-Driven Recovery Rendered Fragile by the Cyclical Downturn in the European Business Climate

All throughout the nineties it was exports that had propelled growth in the furniture industry. In Hungary, nearly 50 per cent of the production was exported to European countries in the year 2000. In Poland the percentage was even higher : 80 per cent of the furniture manufactured was exported (half of it to Germany), or 6.7 per cent of the total Polish exports in 2000. With regard to France, Romania is its 12th biggest furniture supplier (78 million euros in 1999), at par with Indonesia, whereas Poland ranks 14th among its partners. Hungary and Poland have benefited from the renewed vitality of the sector in Europe after some difficult years during the period 1991-1997.

The evolution of the CEECs' comparative advantages in the furniture field stands out clearly during the period 1993-1999. Based on an evaluation of the trade balance ratio of this sector to the trade balance of total products, a recent analysis by CEPII shows that furniture has remained in second position, taking the seven strong points of this zone[69] as a referent. Its stagnation around 10 per cent of the overall trade balance indicates that other sectors such as automobiles and electronics are henceforth more dynamic. Nevertheless, the CEECs' share in the global import of furniture from the EU has gone up from 7.6 per cent to 12.3 per cent between 1993 and 1999, i.e. in the second position just after clothing.

This evolution of a singularly specialised activity, characterized by sub-contracting, needs to be qualified. An integral part of sub-contracting is the import of raw materials and especially of components that are transformed and then re-exported. Germany and Italy are at the heart of this process, especially the latter, which is the

69. Mohammed Hedi Bchir, Mathilde Maurel, 'Impacts économiques et sociaux de l'élargissement pour l'Union européenne et la France', op. cit.

biggest furniture exporter of Europe, while the former is Europe's biggest buyer.

In Poland's case, furniture-making is a business activity that cannot be ignored. Representing nearly half the exports of the zone, its comparative advantage has continued to improve and has become the country's principal strong point from 1996, while its sales have gone up from 3.5 per cent to 6.4 per cent of the EU's global import of furniture. To this we have to add the 'woodworks' sector, which went up from 3.15 to 5.6 per cent of EU imports. However, if the relative dependence of its neighbours on furniture exports is less, their dynamism seems to be greater. Between 1995 and 1999, Hungary has thus achieved an export growth of +143 per cent, the Czech Republic + 93 per cent and Poland + 67 per cent. This is indicative of the neighbourhood effect exerted by Germany, Austria and Italy on the sub-contracting operations. Inversely, some sectors were partially phased-out towards the middle of the decade in Bulgaria and Romania, especially in the second half, when furniture sales of the six principal CEECs were reduced by more than 50 per cent and dropped to 10 per cent in 2000. This factor highlights the fact that in this sector also the wage level is far from being the principal determinant. The growing stability in Romania, both on the political as well as the economic front, with the appearance of a substantial wage differential, on the contrary reversed the trend in the beginning of 2000.

These export figures illustrate the competitiveness of the firms of some countries of the zone but also the growing dependency vis-à-vis West European markets, which can make them more vulnerable, especially in this sector. As a matter of fact, furniture is an area where the effect of the periods of growth and slowdown of consumption are amplified. The recessional trend prevailing in the European markets since 2001 have forced some of the region's firms into a difficult position. For example, the Czech firm Tusculum, one of the biggest manufacturers of decorative furniture[70], reduced its workforce by 10 per cent in 2002. This firm, which exports 95 per cent of its production to Germany was extremely hard hit by the reduction in the demand for furniture in that country. In early 2002, the firms of

---

70. Utilitarian and decorative furniture in homes (tapestry, beds, tables, clocks....).

the entire zone similarly announced a reduction in their workforce in order to lower production costs and remain competitive in the eventuality of a further decline in activity.

However, Central Europe continues to attract foreign investors, mostly European, as we can see from the frequent advertisements announcing the opening of factories. Geographical proximity and low production costs are the undeniable advantages that the CEECs possess. Pressure on costs during a cyclical reversal can act in favour of other countries of the region, such as Romania or the western Balkan states, where the political and macro-economic climate is much more stable now. The phenomenon of the 'flight of wild geese' that we mentioned in the section on textiles is repeated here. In view of the setback to the European markets, the CEECs consider it advisable to diversify their export zones by attacking new markets, such as the Middle East or Japan, as the Czech firm TON tried to do. By diversifying the buyer countries, the CEECs try to limit the effects of the decline in European demand. But the dual competition (Asian for the low-end range and West European for the up-market range) limits room to manoeuvre. On the other hand, the domestic markets are starting to offer serious opportunities.

Domestic Markets – New Opportunities for Local Firms But also for West European Firms

To compensate for the decline in exports, CEEC firms are now banking on their domestic markets, which since the nineties have become much more dynamic despite tough competition from west European firms. After years of generally missing out on original products, East European consumers are now looking for interesting designs to refurbish their home and replace old furniture. Demand is fast growing and is attracting local producers who had earlier completely ignored it during the difficult years of transition. It has now become feasible to propose a much wider range of products in the CEECs because of the increase in their household purchasing power.

The major European retailers have since long understood the advantages and the prospects of these markets. Ikea is already well established in the Czech Republic, Poland and Hungary, but competition is also beginning to emerge. The Austrian firm Kika in

Hungary, the German firm Roller in Poland and the French firm Conforma, are keen to take advantage of these markets, which already represent 650 million euros in Poland and 177 million in Hungary (however, the furniture market in France is valued at 15 billion). The arrival of these big retailers on the scene has completely restructured the retail market and radically changed the consumption pattern. It is now easier for a European exporter to find a retailer even if competition is keen, especially from German or Italian groups that had established their presence on these markets at least 5 years ago.

In Poland, the principal sources of supply are Germany (32 per cent of Polish imports), Italy (21 per cent) and France (8 per cent). The reasons for France lagging behind (but not all French companies that for commercial or logistical reasons can export from Germany or from their manufacturing bases in the region) are interesting. According to some surveys, there are certain cliches attributed to French furniture by importers who recognise its good quality but consider it as being too original and too elegant for current CEEC taste. Also it has not achieved the price-competitiveness of the Italian and German competitors (this last element is especially a handicap for new markets). This explains why the turnover of firms producing fine furniture, such as Ligne Roset, is bigger in Russia than in the CEECs as a whole, given the category of rich consumers who are to be found in big cities like Moscow, Saint-Petersburg and even Novossibirsk.

However, the direct consequence of the increase in consumers' purchasing power in the CEECs is that domestic demand has become much more quality and design conscious and is asking for the more up-market range of products. In Poland, growth forecasts for home furniture have predicted a doubling of sales within the next ten years. The furniture industry of the region is, moreover, closely linked to investments in the construction sector, which is expected to flourish in the next few years so as to satisfy the present housing shortage. The CEECs' lagging behind Western Europe in the furniture sector could thus be overcome in the next 15 years. The integration of some of the countries with the EU should accelerate this process, as Spain and Portugal succeeded in doing after they joined.

NICT (or IT, Information Technologies): The Difficult Conversion of Supply and the Unequal Convergence of Demand

The Stockholm European Council, in March 2001, stressed the urgency of mobilising Europe's vast potential in the new information and communication technology (NICT) related sectors. The latter entail infrastructural investment for generating growth, eventual significant productivity gains for firms, but also a business turnover directly linked to household consumption, firstly in terms of equipment and secondly in terms of recurrent consumption. What is the position of the candidate countries in view of the challenge posed by supply and demand?

A Promising Beginning Interrupted by the Internet Bubble Crisis of the Second Millennium

In early 2002, Bill Gates announced Microsoft's entry into the games console market hitherto dominated by Sony, Nintendo and Sega (10 million euros). It was a first for this group, whose forte till now had been software rather than hardware. However, its manufacturing venture was initially limited to the development of the *Xbox*. For costing reasons, the manufacture of this console was from the start sub-contracted to the electronics giant Flextronics, a firm specialising in the assembly of electronic products. Of Singaporean origin, this sub-contractor whose capital originates equally from American and Singaporean sources, is present in more than forty countries. Two of these countries were supposed to make the *Xbox* : Mexico for the north American market and Hungary for the European continent, where the demand was estimated at one-third of the global market for this console. In Hungary, Flextronics directly owned two factories with a workforce of 7,000 people and sub-contracted in about ten other establishments. This fabulous OEM (Original Equipment Manufacturing) contract would have allowed it to increase its workforce in Hungary. Three months later, Microsoft announced that the production of the *Xbox* was being entirely transferred to China. The games consoles price war had got the better of Hungary's competitiveness and its vague efforts to become Europe's electronic hub, as Ireland had done.

A symbol of globalisation and also of the externalisation that characterises electronics operations, this contract is indicative of the place of the CEECs in this industry at the peak of the internet bubble. A complementary production centre was being developed here since the mid-nineties, which was not intended as an alternative to those that were in existence in Ireland, Wales, and Scotland's 'Silicon Glen'. Since the sixties, these three areas had in effect drawn American and Asian investors in electronics, who wanted to develop closer ties with the European market. A considerable proportion of the electronic goods sold in Europe, particularly computers, are manufactured here.

At the beginning of the nineties, European groups (Philips, Siemens, Thomson) were the first to venture into Central Europe at a time when some of the historic giants of the Comecon were privatised : Telsa in the Czech Republic, Videoton in Hungary and Polkolor in Poland. They were followed by American groups such as IBM and Motorola, Japanese groups, Matsushita and Sony, after which followed the Korean (Samsung), Taiwanese and Singaporean groups. These groups generally preferred to construct new factories in countries situated at the gates of the 'fortress' that was Europe. The proximity of the European markets, the presence of skilled and cheap labour and investor-friendly policies were the ingredients of success in this industry dominated by some fifty firms of international stature.

In 2001, analysts congratulated themselves that there was not much danger for the CEECs if the internet bubble burst. However, this situational economic advantage has a downside : high tech industries even now occupy a rather negligible place in their exports (often less than 10 per cent instead of 30 per cent in France and even more in the Asian countries). The two exceptions are Estonia and especially Hungary, where electronic sales represent nearly 35 per cent of total exports, and this for historical reasons. Within the Comecon, Hungary was responsible for information technology because of its greater trade exposure to the West and its proximity to Vienna, considered at the time to be an important crossroads of industrial espionage. The difficulties encountered in importing West European materials directly led to the development of local manufacturing know-how. Once the Iron Curtain had fallen the great multi-nationals salvaged then exploited these assets, so that Hungary experienced an electronic boom in the nineties. According to the OECD, Hungary was ranked third in the world for job-creation in this sector, and second in terms of contribution to the GDP.

Among the electronic groups present in Hungary today, we find the big multi-nationals such as Philips, General Electric, Compaq, Ericsson, Nokia and Flextronics. However, in 2002 most of them announced a substantial cut in the size of their workforce as a result of the global crisis prevailing in the industry. Both IBM (by as much as half) and Flextronics declared their intention of reducing their workforce. The chances of survival of the Hungarian electronic hub trapped between a triumphant industrial Asia and an old Europe ruling over the R&D (Research and Development) sector, will depend upon its capacity to re-position itself thanks to its pool of systems engineers but also, probably, the potential of the software industry in neighbouring Romania.

On the Hungarian side, the phasing-out of the home electronics segment (including the commonplace products manufactured en masse such as small-sized television sets), in which Asia appears to be unbeatable as market leader, needs to be planned in favour of the allied services, especially logistics. Secondly, R&D centres, more upstream than in the European laboratories, should be set up. Flextronics, IBM, Philips and the former French subsidiary of Framatome, FCI, want to continue to invest in these activities as the salary costs of software engineers is three times lower than in Western Europe.

Romanian specialisation in software could moreover complement and complete electronic development in Hungary. Although still peripheral at the European level, this centre of proficiency associated with a pool of labour-skilled, probably constitutes a good growth potential for Romania. The annual turnover of these companies is approximately 16,300 dollars per employee, or nearly 10 times the per capita GDP. For the EU countries, it is also implies an opportunity in the context of the global shortage of this type of qualification, and checks the ensuing risk of migration from Europe. Alcatel moreover has a factory manufacturing switches at Timisoara, which is gradually becoming a mobile skill development centre for the Balkan region and beyond. Before that, a software development centre had been created, taking to 1200 the number of persons employed by Alcatel in this country. The Siemens group has also chosen the same location, with its Timisoara centre situated opposite Alcatel's.

With a computer experts density five times higher than Russia's and even seven times higher than India's, the quality of human resources on hand in this industry is Romania's prime asset. The country is also sure of renewing this stock of experts as every year approximately 5,000 information technology experts graduate from Romanian universities. The ratio of experts to population is 60 per cent higher than that of the United States (USA). With the gross annual salary of a systems engineer amounting to approximately $12,000 USD per annum, as against $23,000 to $30,000 in Sweden and France and more than $50,000 in the US and Japan, the future is nevertheless uncertain for these CESC (computer engineering and service companies). On the one side their sub-contracting competitiveness and capacity is excellent, on the other brain drain has reached alarming proportions. To this is added a rather mediocre political and business climate in Romania. However, it is interesting to note that the CESC have formed an association in order to give themselves a unique tool for tackling the government. They have thus managed to form quite a powerful lobby to force the authorities to give this sector national priority, which would be an integral part of Romania's accession strategy to the EU, along with very advantageous fiscal benefits.

Although Optimus, a Polish company founded in 1989, was number one in the Polish market in 2000 with 84,000 PCs sold, it was in fact slightly below its 1999 level. Compaq, on the other hand, before the global crisis had announced that it was going to reinforce its presence in the region and get its computers assembled by a local manufacturer, PC Factory. Its objective : to become number one by 2000, ahead of IBM, Dell, Fujitsu-Siemens and Vobis. Compaq seems to have emerged as the regional leader. It is in the lead in Slovakia with a market share of 21 per cent and also in Hungary with 20 per cent, where it is ahead of the Hungarian manufacturer, Albacomp. However, Hewlett Packard bought Compaq out in 2002, but the new group is not doing well at all. The winner in all this is Asia, especially China, where Hewlett Packard has transferred most of its global production. The reasons is quite simple : the scale of production in the CEECs is too small and the domestic markets too limited.

The global players thus do not have many factories in the CEE countries. The branded computers sold in the region come from the EU, mainly Ireland. However, a small beginning was made in the mid-nineties by investing in peripherals (keyboards, screens, printers....etc.). Philips thus produces monitors on a large scale in Hungary : more than 5 million 15 to 19 inch screens between 1997 and 2000. On the other hand, IBM, which also has large production bases in the country, has announced a major reduction of its activities. In reality, the American company did not assemble computers but had a production line of hard disks (6 million pieces since its launch in 1995) in an industrial site rented, including labour, from Videoton, the former regional number one. Hence, its departure has not been too expensive a proposition. The emergence of computer hardware production (the complete range of equipment) in the CEECs in the mid-nineties will perhaps be able to survive the global crisis affecting information technology.

A Slow and Unequal Catching-up of the Demand for NTIC

In the last few years, the development of Mobile (phone) telephony made rapid strides in most countries preparing for accession to the EU. It is true that to start with the level was very low. In five years mobile telephony has progressed from being solely an elite product to a mass one. Apart from characteristics that make it successful world-wide, the mobile telephone paradoxically profits from the low equipment rate of landlines, whose CEEC average went up to 25.7 per 100 persons in 1999, but remained largely below the 54.4 per cent EU average. The number of people with mobile telephones has, on the other hand, risen from 11 million to nearly 30 million between end 1999 and beginning 2001, and the boom that followed in 2002 surprised more than one operator.

One of the reasons for mobile telephony's success (as in several other developing countries) is the high investment cost of installing landlines and the very long waiting period during which the local operator cannot come up with the investment required. In Poland, for example, the installation costs for a land line by the local operator TPSA came to 152 euros for an average per capita wage around 545 euros, whereas the activation of a mobile telephone line came to 33 euros only. The East European consumer thus seems to have given priority to the mobile telephone, generating a sort of a vicious circle in this sector. The subscription and communication rates are increasingly attractive for mobile phones and the speed at which the equipment rate is catching up with the West European level does not conform to the idea of convergence spanning several decades.

Surprisingly this convergence is taking place at a time when West European Telecommunication operators as a whole are feeling the pinch of an 'air pocket' consequent to their huge debts. The latter is combined with a general slowdown, and according to some experts, even suspension of construction of new networks linked to UMTS (Universal Mobile Telecommunications System) licenses or the so-called third generation licenses. Thus there are delays in the scheduled introduction of this new technology in a market now mainly catering to the replacement of equipment, as the mobile diffusion is close to a saturation point.

On the other hand, according to Eurostat, the number of subscribers to mobile phone network providers in the CEECs grew by an average 85 per cent between 1998 and 1999, as against 63 per cent in the EU. It further increased by 42 per cent in 2001, whereas it remained more or less stationary in Western Europe. The equipment ratio in Slovenia and Estonia is respectively 31.5 per cent and 26.8 per cent but 75.8 per cent and 45.5 per cent if we take only the 15 years and above cohort. By comparison, the EU average is respectively 39.1 per cent and 72.4 per cent, a very comparable level. These high rates when compared to the CEEC average (10.7 per cent or 31.27 per cent according to the second indicator are understandable for Slovakia, because of the very high per capita GDP level of the zone (9,300 euros in 1999 for a CEEC average of 3,246 euros) and for Estonia, because of its proximity to the major mobile manufacturers. The Nordic countries, number one in R&D (Research and Development), have in fact localised a part of their assembly units in the Baltic States. By virtue of its size, the configuration of the country and the openness to new technologies of a highly qualified population, Estonia offers the ideal conditions to act as a launching pad for new products : the Wireless Application Protocol[71] was thus

71. A protocol that enables one to connect to the Internet from a mobile telephone.

proposed as early as in 2000 and is available on the three existing networks.

All the Central and Eastern Europe countries cannot claim to have these conditions. If we compare the rate of equipment acquisition of these countries with EU15, the catching-up potential of approximately 30 million subscribers corresponds to the number of actual subscribers multiplied by 2.7. It is thus an important market for European manufacturers at a time when West Europe seems to be taking a rather long 'break'. Moreover, the craze is also raging in countries that are lagging behind such as Romania, because of the lack of fixed telephones. This particular case constitutes a good example of the industrial benefits of enlargement for Western European groups.

The Catching-up of Computer Related Equipment has Slowed Down

The information technology equipment market was estimated at 6 billion euros in 2001 for the CEECs as a whole. This figure is very small when compared to the EU15 (117 billion), which has ten times more PCs. However, to catch up with the American equipment rate (52 per cent in 1999), a challenge for the whole of Europe, means 100 million additional PCs in EU15 and 45 million in the CEECs. But what is the time span we are looking at?

After the introduction of modern computers, banned before, initially the CEEC belt expanded very rapidly. Thus by the end of 2001 they had 12 million PCs and a growth rate, which had been in double digit for several years. With a 40 per cent increase in computer acquisition in 2000, Slovakia also experienced a strong boom : 160,000 units for a computer stock of only 560,000, which by the end of 2001 had become 800,000. Poland represents the biggest regional market with 3.3 million PCs, or as much as the Czech Republic (1.4 million), Hungary (1 million) and Slovakia combined. In reality, it is still nowhere near the European rate of equipment ownership: an average of 8-9 per cent in Central Europe compared to 30.4 per cent in the EU15. Quite logically, Romania has the lowest rate (3.6 per cent) and Slovenia the highest (27.5 per cent), indicating a perfect correlation with per capita income. Poland was just a little more than 8 per cent at the end of 2001. Unlike the mobile telephone, where the growth in the equipment acquisition rate was astonishing, mainly due to household purchases and the low cost of mobiles, the demand for PCs is dominated by professionals, primarily because of regular equipment upgrades by the multinationals present in the region.

Thus catching up with the EU15 level could be a slow process, all the more as computer sales in 2001 were very poor in the CEECs. In Hungary, the progress was merely 1.5 per cent and that too because of purchases by the government and the small and medium enterprises. In Poland, sales dropped by nearly 10 per cent, showing how low individual incomes in Central Europe affect spending especially when it comes to expensive products. For information technologies as a whole, CEEC expenditure in 2001 amounted to a mere 11 billion euros as against 305 billion in the EU. The per capita expenditure in Slovenia and the Czech Republic was the highest, but only 176 and 168 euros respectively as against an average of 777 euros in the EU15. There is no likelihood of a reduction in this gap at least for some years still and it also explains why the electronic industry in the CEECs has failed to establish itself apart from a few isolated cases.

The Adaptation Crisis in the East European Iron and Steel Industry

More than any other sector, iron and steel was the symbol of success of industrialisation in the communist countries. Post-communist transition has been turbulent. In particular in the coal mining sector, associated mainly with metal production, and the entire energy sector, which ever since has been in a state of chronic over-capacity. To give a rough estimate of the volumes involved, let us say that in 2000 the CEEC production had fallen to 30 million tonnes of crude steel (with production capacity more than double), i.e. 3.6 per cent of total global production, as against 50 million or approximately 6 per cent in 1990. The sector still accounts for 8 to 15 per cent of the total industrial output of the CEECs and the same for employment. This partly explains the vicious circle that restructuring has to contend with in this branch : overstaffing renders privatisation politically and socially hazardous, especially in Poland where it is felt that 12,000 metallurgists would suffice instead of the 40,000 still on the rolls (there were 120,000 in the past).

On the trade front, the once strong position of iron and steel has been drastically eroded because of the double impact of trade :

1) Exports continue to decline steadily but still represent 5 to 15 per cent of the total exports of the principal steel producing countries. The European market represents more than half their external outlets but it is itself in a position of chronic over-capacity;

2) Paradoxically imports have been increasing rapidly : the current market demand has progressed from 3 to 5 per cent per annum as against only 1 per cent in the EU. The unitary value of imports is approximately double that of exports (from high value added steel not locally produced), in particular of products complementary to the new activities that are being developed in Central Europe : automobiles, electrical goods, etc.

On the whole, the CEECs' trade balance in iron and steel is doing an about turn, signaling the end of a historic comparative advantage. In this context, the slow pace of restructuring could compromise the future of this sector permanently as most of the enterprises are not making any profits. For example, in 2001, the deficit of the sole iron and steel company in Hungary, Dunaffer, was approximately 15 million euros. The deficit of probably the most modern enterprise in the region, Kosice in Slovakia, amounted to 177 million dollars in the same year (approximately 180 million euros), while in the Czech Republic only one site showed a profit. These companies are heavily in debt, as for example in Poland, where the total debt amounts to 2.5 billion dollars (about 2.6 billion euros), of which 80 per cent is a short term debt.

This deterioration of the situation is explained by the combination of an outdated production machinery and low productivity (50 per cent of that of the EU, except in Slovakia). In Poland's case, for example, the potential buyers of the four principal steelworks estimate that the total investment needed would be around 1 billion euros. In Slovakia, the last country to set up steelworks, the investment plan for Kosice by the American buyer US Steel, was suspended in the beginning of 2002 because of US trade policy. The protectionist measures implemented by the Bush administration threatened a new steel war. These investments are of course absolutely necessary in order to re-position production, which is still based on low quality products and is not very dynamic in terms of demand. Here we are referring to long products (58 per cent of Polish production capacity) in contrast to flat products (65 per cent of Romanian exports) used in making automobiles and electrical goods, or special steel that is increasingly being used by all industries.

The new global steel crisis can either block the restructuring process because of a substantial world-wide over-capacity, or on the contrary accelerate it if foreign investors take advantage of their position of strength to acquire cheaply the new installations situated at the periphery of the premier world iron and steel market. However, the chances of this happening are quite small. Why would large investments be made in a deteriorating economic climate when the advantages of localisation (locally available raw materials) are slight ? In view of the key factors affecting competitiveness in modern steel production (i.e. heavy inputs of capital and technology), it seems doubtful that the CEECs can emerge as large winners in the new deal in this industry. The restructuring plans demanded by the European Commission, which have to be effectively signed before accession, will have to be strictly applied. If not, safeguard clauses will be activated, as defined by the Copenhagen European Council in 2002. These clauses are aimed at rationalising the production capacities of Greater Europe, which translates as the immediate reduction of excess capacity, estimated at nearly 50 per cent. In this context the remaining iron and steel mills will mainly be used to feed the few dynamic industrial sectors that are the large consumers of steel, such as automobiles or the engineering industry. It seems unlikely that they will remain major exporters to West Europe.

The Emergence of a New Automobile Hub in Europe

While the automobile sales in the CEECs picked up again from the mid-nineties after a drop of more than 70 per cent in 1990-1992, they sustained another setback as a result of the Polish market crisis. After a decline in sales by 15.4 per cent in 2000, the trend persisted in 2001 (-12 per cent), dropping from a little less than 1 million cars sold in 2000 to 870,000, as against 14.4 million in the EU15. The difference in the size of markets is significant even if sales in 2002 were restored to their 1996 level. It is a good illustration of the dangers of false illusions that exist in these emerging European markets. What we have here is an unequivocal basic trend : a convergence with the West European rate of equipment acquisition. But the constraints of time and money also play a role, as automobiles fall into the expensive category. However, international manufacturers capitalize on the competitive short-term supply factor to establish a sustainable presence in a region with a strong potential in the medium term. In this sector, the European landscape will change considerably with enlargement, but its magnitude should not be exaggerated.

The Offensive Strategies of the Principal Manufacturers are of a Pan-European Nature

Towards the end of December 2001, PSA(Peugeot Automobile) and Toyota announced the construction of a joint factory at Kohlin, near Prague with the aim of assembling 300,000 vehicles per annum. The introductory model would target the small car market in Europe but would focus on the CEEC region. This decision, which represents an investment of 1 billion euros in 2005, is part of a trend characterised by three factors in the Central European context.

The first factor is the reinforced specialisation of some eastern European countries. Five of them (Czech Republic, Poland, Slovakia and Slovenia) are responsible for 75 per cent of the trade in this sector with the EU15, which is mainly divided between Germany (52 per cent), Italy (12.5 per cent) and France (11 per cent). In these countries the automobile branch, and in particular components, accounted for 15 to 20 per cent of exports in 2001. The 'individual cars' category has demonstrated a surplus since 1998, but CEE countries are net importers of components. Actually, one can notice different types of specialisation. Integration is of the horizontal type in Hungary, which is traditionally strong in motors (more than a million units produced by the Audi factory in Györ) and where components can depend on its other strong points such as electronics and plastics. On the other hand, integration is more vertical in the Czech Republic, where since 1895 Skoda has been the keystone of this country's comparative advantage. There was, however, an increasing surplus of components in relation to the rest of the world[72]. This is

72. This signifies that initially cars were manufactured, then steel and flat glass, for they are needed in automobile production. It is also called industrialisation by induction.

not the case with Slovakia where the agglomeration phenomenon involving motor vehicle equipment manufacturers is not seen on a large scale, although the Volkswagen assembly plants in Bratislava produces more than 300,000 cars today (mainly the *Polo*). Slovenia is more like a workshop, where the share of component imports have increased proportionally with automobile exports (Renault being the only exporter in reality), i.e. an increase of 50 per cent approximately between 1995 and 1998. Despite the large investments and an official will to procure comparative advantages in the automobile field by taking advantage of the asset that its domestic market represents, Poland still has a comparative disadvantage in the two automobile branches and in components. It owes its absolute weight to the size of its domestic market. However, the rapid rise of car imports in a market gradually losing its protected status, is likely to herald a new phase of re-specialisation, this time in the field of and components.

In the second place, the strategies of firms towards central Europe are clearly defined in the pan-European context. On the demand side the size of the markets *a priori* hardly justifies heavy investments, while the over-capacity in Western Europe is around 40 per cent. The registration of new cars in the CEEC, in 2001, was around 7 per cent of those in EU15, i.e. perhaps twice as less in terms of value as the cars here are smaller and correspond to the bottom end of the range. Recent evolution does not indicate that the catching-up has been significant : +3.1 per cent per annum in the CEECs between 1996 and 2000, as against + 3.7 per cent in the EU15. Lastly, catching-up with the West European rate of equipment acquisition only represents a cumulated total stock of 10 million cars, i.e. nine months of registration in the West! Manufacturers world-wide competing with each other for the smallest space in this game of Go[73], which is what the automobile sector has become, cannot overlook the annual demand, which all experts estimate will be around 2.5 million units in 2010, i.e. the equivalent of the French market. Hence, one of the best strategies consists of profiting today from the comparative advantages of production in the zone to prepare for tomorrow's sales.

73. Well-known Chinese game played on a checkerboard on which each player tries to increase as much as possible the space that he controls by carefully placing his pieces one by one on the board. All the major industries of the world operate in the same way.

Figure 4.3

Evolution of the CEECs' Share in the EU27 Supply and Demand for Car in 2000 and 2010 (estimtes)

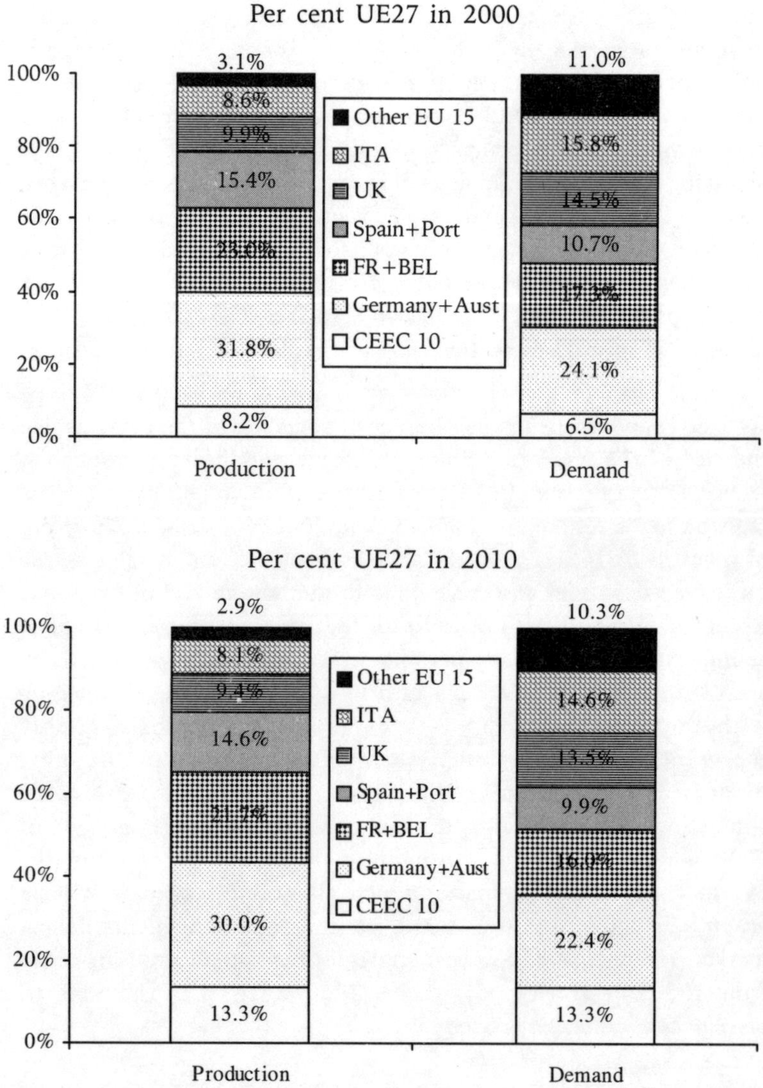

Source: Boillot J.J., Lepape Y. (2002), Le renouveau de l'industrie automobile dans les pays d'Europe centrale et orientale, Edition CFCE

On the supply side, although technologically backward, the region yet boasts of several automobile factories. Right from the nineties some were already closely associated with European manufacturers such as Volkswagen, Fiat and Renault[74]. On narrow markets the position of the first entrant confers a decisive advantage, hence the fierce competition : Renault with Revoz in Slovenia and Dacia in Romania, Volkswagen with Skoda in the Czech Republic and Fiat in Poland. In the context of Greater Europe, although the strategic contribution may appear small in volume, it nevertheless generally helps to consolidate a firm's pan-European position. For example Renault with 11.3 per cent of the market share in the CEECs and 10.6 per cent in the EU, and Volkswagen with respectively 23.7 and 18.7 per cent. The good local brands in effect have a tendency to remain top sellers in their own country: At the end of 2001, Skoda could still claim 50 per cent and 54 per cent of the Slovakian and Czech markets, and Dacia more than 60 per cent in Romania. Without an industrial presence in the area, PSA's 9 per cent market share in the CEEC zone was a laudable achievement... hence Kohlin's decision to allow the French group to increase its stake to 15 per cent of the pan-European market share by the year 2005.

Lastly, the PSA-Toyota operation confirms the dynamic effects of localisation in the form of specialised clusters, which profit from three factors : the proximity of large European markets along the communication axes connecting the Western and Easterns parts of continental Europe; the existence of a specialised workforce combined with imported modern technologies ensuring productivity potentially higher than the European average, as in Hungary (124 per cent) or the Czech Republic (101 per cent); lastly, government incentives by way of taxes and more importantly assistance in training labour, in logistics, or in providing the necessary support to site base preparation. In this instance, PSA and Toyota have benefited from an industrial site initially prepared for BMW, but which eventually chose the Leipzig region for political (crisis in former GDR) and economic (substantial government aid via the European Commission) reasons.

---

74. Xavier Richet, Frédéric Bourassa, "The Re-emergence of the Automotive Industry in Eastern Europe," in Christian von Hirschhausen, Jürgen Bitzer (eds.), The Globalization of Industry and Innovation in Eastern Europe: *From Post-Socialist Restructuring to International Competitiveness*, Edward Elgar Publishing, Cheltenham (United Kingdom), Northampton (United States), 2000, pp. 59-94.

No Major Upheaval in the European Automobile Market, but a Challenge

On a pan-European level, a new pole has thus emerged in central Europe. Does this entail an upheaval or a shift in the economic geography? In terms of quantities, 1.3 million personal cars were produced in the region as against 2.2 million in Spain and 3.1 million in France in 2002. The new projects identified as of today should take the production capacity of the CEECs to at least 2.5 millions units in the next ten years. This corresponds to the emergence of a set-up similar to the Iberian hub (Spain and Portugal). Although this will lead to greater competition within Europe, the formation of a new automobile pole in the CEECs is in line with the continentalisation of automobile localisation. This is in contrast to geographical concentration in one or two centres, as in the North American model where the automobile industry is largely concentrated around the Great Lakes. The reorganisation of the European automobile map by 2010 shows a slight reinforcement of the relative weight of the CEE countries, both with regard to supply as well as demand. In terms of the trade balance, the distortion is slight. On the other hand, the intensification of competition in this large market induces each territory and producer to find a niche on the new matrix range-competitiveness of the production sites. Where will we produce tomorrow and more efficiently, which models are most in demand and for what markets? A challenge that the emergence of the Central European (and Turkish) automobile hub only accentuates further. Hence the hypersensitivity to certain localisation plans in the CEEC, in particular on the part of some automobile equipment manufacturers, who obviously prefer to follow their partners instead of relocating the totality of their production.

In view of this challenge, the French manufacturers want to take advantage of the situation while the going is good, each one developing an original strategy founded on the same innovative, competitive and commercially dynamic base. Renault has spun its pan-European web, which includes the Slovenia-Romania-Turkey triangle (140,000 cars in its Bursa factory, including the famous *Clio trois corps*, which is being massively exported to the CEEC). The development of a truly European site in Romania should enable it to overtake Fiat. Moreover, this location will see the first 'world car' ever produced in a former communist country (it will be introduced in India in 2006). PSA, for its part, has surprised all market analysts. In 2002, its commercial progress placed it in the third position in a region where it had no local industrial presence. The success of the *206* and of *Xsara* shows that the transport costs and the entry barriers for the CEECs are very like those of other European countries. By setting up a production base in the CEECs, PSA will be in an area that other competitors could prevent it from occupying.

Figure 4.4

Trade Between France and CEECs in the Automotive Sector 1991-2002

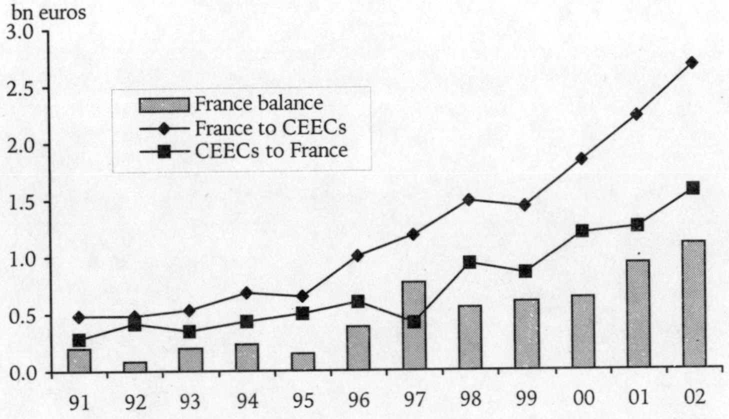

Source: French Customs

In fact, the enlargement experience of the eighties in Spain and Portugal shows that French trade in the entire automobile sector has largely benefited from the virtuous sequence of integration. There is greater cross trade with the new markets in the process of catching-up, and a positive balance of trade, which is on the rise especially when French manufacturers make the effort to innovate, as is actually the case. More painful perhaps, the same process has been followed by Germany with a concentration of very top-end cars in Germany itself and the shift to eastern Europe for the medium to low end segments.

5

India and EU Enlargement: Challenges and Opportunities[75]

Economic Implications of EU Enlargement

With 25 member-states and nearly 460 million citizens with high purchasing power, European Union is India's largest potential market. While the enlargement of EU is expected to lead to an improvement in the trade access to the accession nations and strengthen India-EU trade linkages further, it is also likely to reduce or eliminate the barriers to the movement of goods and services, labor and capital between these countries. This would, in turn, result in an enlarged single EU market with its impact on the investment patterns, inbound as well as outbound.

EU Enlargement and its Impact on India-EU Trade Linkages

EU is India's largest trading partner, accounting for 25 per cent of India's global trade. Bulk of India's exports to EU-15 consists of non-manufactured/semi-manufactured products in the sectors of Textiles, Leather product, Chemicals, Agricultural products, etc. A major part of exports/imports is concentrated with UK, Belgium and Germany. As far as India's trade with the Accession Countries is concerned, currently India's exports are mainly concentrated with Poland, followed by Czech Republic. The share of the other accession countries is very low. The Czech Republic has the largest share in India's total imports from the accession countries, accounting for 37 per cent of the same. Trade between India and the accession countries is currently below potential, mainly because of the inadequate commercial arrangements (correspondent banking, lines of credit,

75. A special thank for this chapter prepared by the Federation of Indian Chambers of Commerce and Industry (FICCI), New Delhi.

export guarantee, insurance, trade documentation and legalization procedures) to facilitate trade payments, inadequate trade links, air routes, visa and consular arrangements. Hence, greater bilateral arrangements with these countries are needed to ease the trade relations between India and these countries.

Enlargement of EU would have its impact on India-EU trade linkages. The overall impact of accession on India's trade can be divided into two effects:

Figure 5.1

India's Exports to the EU in 2002-03 Country-wise Distribution

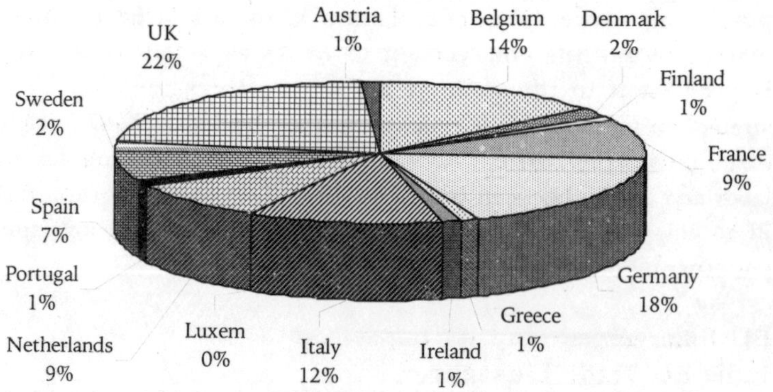

Figure 5.2

India's Imports from EU in 2002-03 Country-wise Distribution

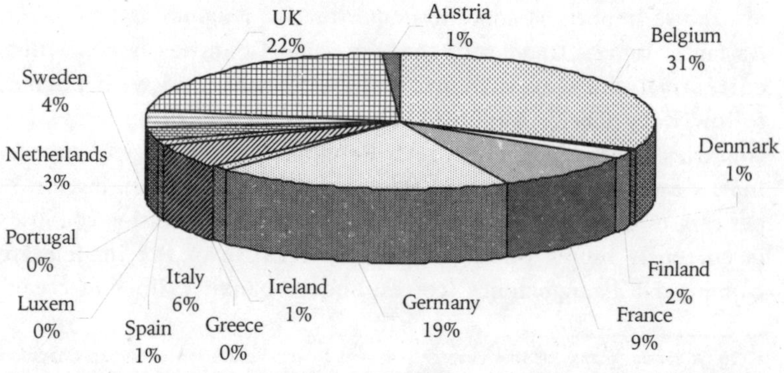

Source: DGCI&S

Figure 5.3

India's Exports to Accession Countries('02-'03)
Country-wise Distribution

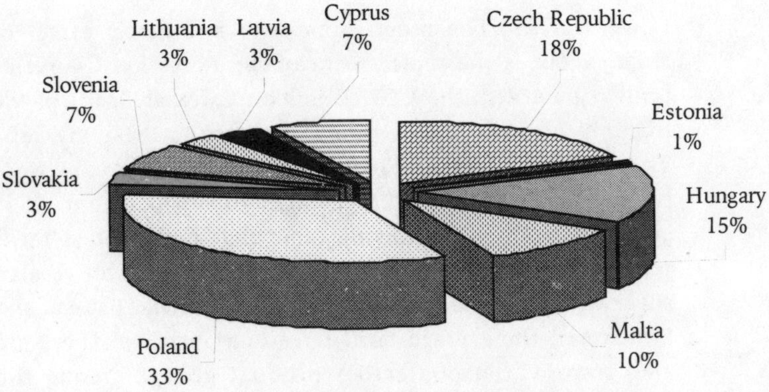

Figure 5.4

India's Imports from Accession Countries('02-'03)
Country-wise Distribution

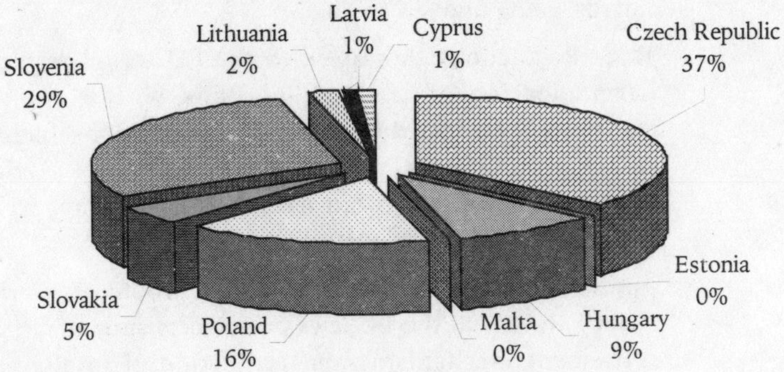

Source: DGCI&S

Trade Creation Effect: Trade creation occurs when imports from a new, efficient member replace inefficient local production. In the case of EU-India trade after enlargement, trade creation is seen as a possibility due to the following reasons:

- Enlarged Market: An enlarged EU represents market expansion with a population of more than 455 million (an increase of 85 million), a GDP of 10 trillion euros representing around 20 per cent of world's trade.
- Lower Tariffs: The most immediate and direct effect of enlargement is the replacement of the Accession Countries tariff regime with the CET (Common External Tariff) of the EU, which alters India's terms of access to these markets. The weighted average tariffs in accession countries were higher than the EU average tariff of 3.6 per cent. It is apparent from the following table that the greatest tariff reductions apply for Poland and Hungary. Table 1 also suggests that in the case of Baltic states (Latvia, Estonia and Lithuania), the average tariff rates may increase. There are also some variations across product groups among the countries themselves. Therefore, the tariff effects would be different for each member.
- EU Regulations Applicable to Accession Countries: Accession is expected to lead to an improvement in the trade access to these nations also on account of the EU standards being applied to them.
  - Trade Regulations: Accession to the EU would result in harmonization of trade regulations within a given transition periods. Some of these regulations include customs procedures, testing, certification and product approvals, all of which can have a significant impact on the business environment in these locations.
  - Applicability of EU Laws: Accession would also bring about harmony in the EU laws on subjects such as dispute settlement mechanisms and protection of intellectual property rights, which can have a major trade creation potential.

Trade Diversion Effect: Trade diversion is defined as a shift of imports from an efficient to a less-efficient source (and occurs, for example, when imports from a non-member country are replaced by imports from a new member). Where trade liberalization involves removing barriers to selected countries only, as it occurs under a

Table 5.1

Estimated Simple Average MFN Applied Tariffs (ACs & EU) in Percentage

	Cyprus	*Czech Republic*	*Estonia*	*Hungary*	*Lithuania*	*Latvia*	*Malta*	*Poland*	*Slovenia*	*Slovak Republic*	*EU*
Total	9.7	6.0	3.2	11.7	5.1	4.2	6.2	15.2	8.8	6.0	6.3
Non-agricultural	4.6	4.2	0.1	7.3	2.3	2.0	5.9	10.3	7.9	4.2	4.0
Industrial	3.8	4.4	0.0	7.0	2.3	1.7	5.9	9.8	8.0	4.4	3.6
Agricultural	31.1	13.5	14.9	30.9	14.6	13.0	7.4	34.6	13.3	13.1	16.2

Source: FICCI

preferential trading agreement such as the European enlargement, trade diversion effects may to some extent, offset the trade creation effects. This occurs when member-countries displace tariff-ridden imports from non-member regions with tariff-free imports from other members, even though the replacing imports may be more expensive to produce. The diversionary impact of enlargement of the European Union for India may come in the form of greater competition from the accession countries in those commodities in which both India and the accession countries are suppliers to the West European markets. Some of these products include footwear, leather & leather products, automotive components, synthetic yarn, furniture, etc. Among the accession nations, Poland and the Czech Republic are our main competitors. Poland competes with India in 46 of its top 100 exports to EU, and Czech competes in 34 items. A major area of concern for India is that the acceding countries would have a tariff advantage over India, which currently attracts GSP tariffs ranging from 4 per cent to 100 per cent. As a result, Indian exports in several important categories are likely to lose competitive price advantage on account of tariffs as well as lower shipment costs from accession countries.

EU Enlargement and its Impact on India-EU Investment Linkages

Among the accession countries, more than 70 per cent of the investments into India have come from the Czech Republic during 1991-2003. The Czech Republic has established a large number of industrial projects in India in the fields of energy, metallurgy, machine tools and in defense. Accession might lead to greater competition for inbound FDI since there are number of locations in the accession countries that offer the same low-cost advantages as India. However, it is also possible that due to the accession into the EU, there could be large movements of skilled and unskilled labour from accession countries to the West European nations. This may result in increase in the cost of labour, depriving them of their competitive advantage over India. Labour costs may also rise as a result of the new EU labour laws and employment regulations that would apply to the accession countries. In such a scenario, Indian companies could gain by becoming an attractive destination for FDI inflows. The enlargement of the European Union would also provide an opportunity for Indian business houses to enter into alliances and joint ventures in sectors such as automobile, chemicals and pharmaceuticals, machinery and equipment, electronics, exploration of oil and natural gas, power stations and food processing sectors and IT (or IT Information Technologies). Indian business houses can look at setting up bases in the accession countries to cater well to the entire EU market. The overall business climate in the accession countries may also improve due to the EU standards being applied to these countries.

Figure 5.5

FDI into India from EU from 1991 to 2003
Country-wise Distribution

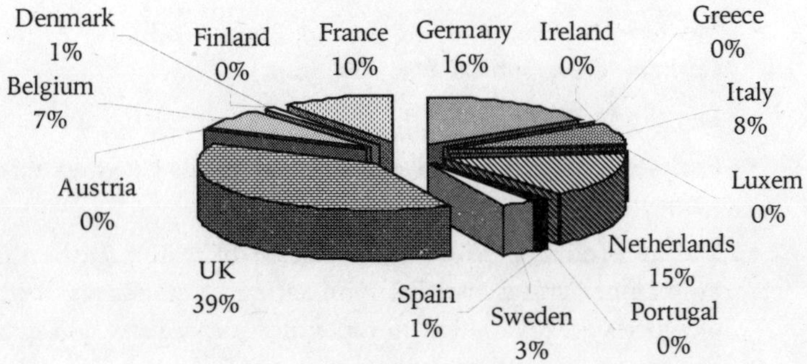

Figure 5.6

FDI into India from Accession Countries from 1991 to 2003
Country-wise Distribution

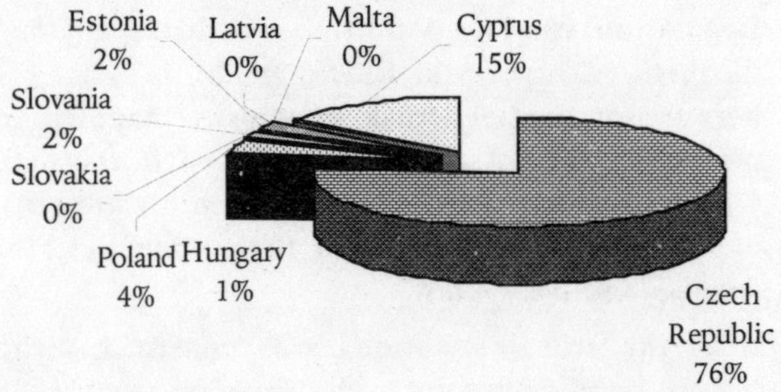

Source: SIA, Ministry of Industrial Policy & Promotion, New Delhi July 2004

Analysis of the Keys Sectors

Agriculture and Allied Products

The European Union has evolved as a major destination for India's agricultural items. The total exports of agri food items to the EU during 2002-03 were around $ 255 mn, while for USA, these were close to $ 200 mn. However, due to a number of constraints involving anti-dumping and non-tariff barriers by the EU, the full potential of Indo-EU trade in food and processed food products has not been realized. EU members remain one of the most frequent users of trade defense mechanism, including anti-dumping duties and countervailing duties. Some of these constraints include:

- Tea, Coffee, Fruits, Vegetables- Pesticide residues more stringent than Codex standards.
- Meat, Milk Products, Bone and Bone Products, Animal Casings- Geographical BSE risk status.
- Egg Products- Delay in the approval of exporting units.
- Fruits and Vegetables- Pesticides/chemicals residues more stringent
- Marine Products- Non-harmonization of testing/inspection by member states, non-harmonization of standards set by member-states, variation in rapid alert procedures and delay in the approval of the exporting units.
- Organic Products- Delay in notifying and accepting Indian standards for organic products.
- Spirits, Wines and Whisky- In spirits, one of the non-tariff barriers is the EU Council's definition of whisky under Regulation 15. The definition of whisky at one stroke disqualified exports of whisky made in India, primarily because of the feedstock of whisky made in India is molasses, and not grain as prescribed in the definition. Other non-tariff barriers, which inhibit growth of our exports of Indian whisky to their countries, relate to labeling and pack sizes.

As far as the acceding nations are concerned, although a substantial part of India's exports to the accession countries is in the traditional products, food items have remained largely negligible in the export basket. India's exports to the acceding nations was a mere $11 mn during 2002-03. In this region, a substantial portion of trade is with Poland, accounting for around 61 percent of India's exports to ACs in agricultural products. The enlargement may provide an opportunity for Indian exporters of farm products since the integration of CEEC into the EMU will facilitate easy exploration of the yet untapped markets and make planning easier for a larger common market with only one currency, one set of rules and administrative procedures. In order to tap this potential, there is a need to integrate all the elements of food supply chains, to create markets, to build brands and follow the right market strategies.

Information Technology

Indian information technology is regarded as the sunrise sector of the Indian economy with software services exports surging ahead from $2.2 billion in 1998-99 to $ 9.6 billion during 2002-03. Region-wise the following is the break up of IT services. As is evident from the above table, North America has the largest share in India's total exports of IT services. Although the market share of the Western European region is merely 21 percent, exports with this region are expected to rise especially after the visa quota reductions for IT professionals in USA. The presence of Indian IT services in Europe is below potential largely due to the wide variations within European markets in terms of differences in language and culture. This requires a different market strategy for different countries within Europe. The problem compounds with the acceding nations due to lack of knowledge of each other's markets. However, enlargement can be seen as a good opportunity for Indian IT companies, especially in the following context:

- The existing European nations, especially UK, have shown keen interest in gaining from the opportunities arising from outsourcing from India.
- In the current scenario, there is a considerable security concern among the European nations for their airports etc. There is immense scope for Indo-EU partnership in strengthening their existing security systems with the help of Indian IT expertise in developing similar systems.

- There is also a need for India and the New Europe to join hands in streamlining the laws and taxation system for the promotion of E-business.

Table 5.2

IT Services Spending: Regional Shares, 2002-03

Region	*IT Services Spending (USD bn)*	*India's Exports (USD mn)*	*India's Market Share (%)*	*Relative Dependence Ratio*	*Share in India's Exports*
North America	171.1	6,685	3.92	1.4	67.7
Western Europe	109.6	2,103	1.92	0.7	21.3
Latin America & Rest of world	17.5	583	3.33	1.2	5.9
Asia Pacific	16.0	311	1.94	0.7	3.2
Total	349.1	9,875	2.82		100

Source: Nasscom

Textile and Clothing

The textile and clothing sector holds a very important position for India. It is the largest export earner for our nation and the largest employment generator. EU and the USA are the largest export destinations. The EU, being the largest trader of textile and clothing, assumes special significance. Around 40 percent of India's textiles and clothing exports go to the EU and India's share in EU's imports is around 7 percent.

As far as the accession countries are concerned, their exports of textile and clothing are also heavily dependent on the EU market. In the post-quota regime, competition is likely to rise for the Indian exporters from other non-member countries like China. Accession countries may not pose a major competition in this sector since they already have unrestricted access to the market. However, the accession countries would still have advantage over India since our exports to EU attract a Generalized System of Preferences (GSP) tariff ranging from 4-11 per cent. In view of the potential for India to capture a larger market share after enlargement and in the post quota regime, it is important that the current fragmented structure of the industry should be strengthened with a greater focus on improving seed quality and cotton productivity to improve quality cotton availability. The labour and land laws also need to be amended.

Pharmaceuticals

Pharmaceuticals and allied chemicals are our sunrise industry with a bright future. Our industry is globally very competitive and our domestic companies are fast emerging as prominent players in the world markets. Our exports to the EU and all the candidate countries are quite substantial in this sector. The enlargement of the EU is going to open further opportunities in this sector. Most of the EU members are already looking at India as a big supplier in this sector because of the low cost and local talent available in this industry. The medical facilities, research costs and labour costs are among the lowest in the world. In the pharma sector, there is not much threat of competition from the acceding nations in the West European market. The low-cost advantage of the accession countries may no longer remain since they would have to comply with a large number of EU regulations including their licensing rules that might jack up their costs. However, in the case of generic products, the enlargement would benefit the accession countries since there would be easier registration of generic products. The success of this sector depends on the way in which we are able to manage the new IPR regime under the WTO. There are a lot of products whose Indian clones are much cheaper than the original products patented by foreign companies. The industry should now invest heavily in research and development activities and come up with their original products and obtain patents for them.

Table 5.3

Comparative Cost Between Europe and India in Pharmaceuticals

	Europe	*India*
Cost of developing a molecule	$ 10-20 million	$ 1.4-2 million
Salary of a chemist with a Ph.D	$ 100,000	$ 15,000

Source: FICCI

India and the New Europe: Issues and Challenges

Enlargement of the European Union has thrown up a wide gamut of opportunities for countries like India. According to the respondents to the FICCI survey on 'India–CEE Trade Linkages, Opportunities and Challenges', India's trade volume with the accession countries can easily be doubled in less than three years. There are great opportunities as there would now be uniform trade regulations, uniform duty structure and common technical specification in those countries that have joined the European Union. However, to capitalize on the above opportunities, the following issues need to be addressed:

Composition of India's Export Basket: The current trade figures reveal that the basket of commodities of export to the EU are largely traditional products such as food and food products, gems & jewellery, clothing & textiles, marine products, etc. With India emerging as an IT destination for countries like the US, it would be advantageous for India to look at EU for exporting new-age commodities and services. Some of the potential areas are:

I. Information and communication technology

II. Biotechnology

III. Tourism

IV. Entertainment

V. Urban infrastructure

Low Level of Awareness: There is a general lack of awareness of the potential of trading with the Central and Eastern European states. This inhibits the Indian industry from entering the market. In the coming years, the India-EU Business Summits would see participation from the newly acceded countries and this would, therefore, lead to spread of knowledge of each other's markets.

Increased Competition from the Accession Countries: Respondents to the FICCI Survey also mentioned that to some extent intra-EU trade might reduce the opportunities for other countries including India. Indian companies feel that there is a need to upgrade the existing technology, focus on competitive pricing and timely delivery to withstand the increasing competition, especially from the Central and Eastern European nations.

Non-Tariff Barriers: Enlargement may bring about an increasing applicability of non-tariff measures by the EU nations to protect the domestic market. We have to consolidate our position in the existing market and create new markets for all our export products and protect our industry and exporters from unjust regulations.

The FICCI survey on 'India-CEE Trade Linkages, Opportunities & Challenges' brought out some of the problems that the Indian companies have to face while exporting to the Central & East European countries, five of which have joined EU on May 1,2004 and two more would be joining in 2007. As the table shows, 86 per cent of the participating companies said that trade barriers in the form of high import duties and complex customs procedures were acting as a major impediment for them. Further, delays in obtaining visas and work permit for these countries makes it difficult for Indian company officials and workers to travel to these countries and this affects smooth conduct of business – this problem is high on the agenda of 59 per cent of the respondents. 57 per cent of the participating companies also complained about problems related to payments of dues.

Table 5.4

Problems Faced by Indian Companies Exporting to the Central & East European Countries

(Per cent)

		CEE		
		High	*Medium*	*Low*
1	Trade barriers (import duties& customs)	86		14
2	Language & Cultural barriers	14	14	72
3	Labour laws (Compensation package)	29	43	28
4	Security problems concerning payments	57	29	14
5	Work permits & visa problems	59	28	13
6	Competition from local companies	29	56	15
7	Lack of business information	57	29	14

Source: FICCI survey on 'India-CEE Trade Linkages, Opportunities & Challenges', New Delhi 2004

Other specific problems which the respondents have encountered while exporting to Central & East Europe include:

- Difficulty in carrying out company background checks - As per the respondents, since there are new established companies in this region without business track records banks do not have/give any credit report. In the absence of such information or report it becomes extremely risky for Indian businessmen to extend any line of credit.
- Lack of flights: As there is lack of direct flights, business people have to often schedule their trips much in advance. This also increases the time and cost component of trips to these countries.
- Consular problems: It takes a long time to get a visa for these countries. The only exception being those cases where the applicants already have a US Visa, Canadian Visa and/or Schengen Visa. There is no consistency in the period for which is visa granted in some of these countries.

Recommendations

The FICCI survey on India-CEE trade Linkages, Opportunities & Challenges' highlighted the need for the Indian companies to take the following steps to capitalize on the opportunities thrown open by the enlargement of EU.

- Setting up/establishing offices in the accession countries
- Joining hands with joint venture partners for production and/or marketing
- Appointing agents for introducing and familiarizing Indian products in these markets
- Developing regular contacts through participation in buyer-seller meets
- Enlisting in the local trade directories and advertising in the local trade journals and media
- Creating greater awareness about Indian products by participating in all their trade fairs

The respondents to the survey conducted by FICCI indicated the sectors where technical and/or financial collaboration is possible between India and the Central and East European Countries, including the five accession countries. These sectors include:

- Automobile sector
- Steel
- Information Technology
- Food Processing
- Banking
- Heavy Equipment and Machinery
- Defense Equipments
- Metallurgy & Exploration activities in Hydrocarbon, Gas,Oil
- Aviation sector
- Power projects
- Architectural & Engineering Services
- Construction

Table 5.5

Brief Summary of Accession Countries

Country	*Population*	*GDP (PPP basis) in billion dollars*	*GDP per capita (PPP basis)*	*India's total trade in million (2002-03) dollars*	*Major items of from India*	*Major items of imports exports into India*
Cyprus	771,657	9.4 (2001 est)	16,000 (2001 est)	26.24	Chemicals and pharmaceuticals, food products, cotton, iron and steel	
Czech Republic	10,249,246	157.1 (2002 est)	15,300 (2002 est)	142.9	Cotton, clothing and textiles, electrical machinery and equipment, leather and leather products, chemicals and pharmaceuticals	Vehicles, organic chemicals, minerals, nuclear reactors, machinery and equipment
Poland	38,622,660	373.2 (2002 est)	9,7	144.49	Chemicals and pharmaceuticals, cotton and textile, leather and leather products	Electrical machinery and equipment, nuclear reactors, ships, boats and floating structures, electrical machinery and equipment
Slovenia	1,935,677	37.06 (2002 est)	19,2	94.38	Electrical machinery and equipment, plastic, organic chemicals	Nuclear reactors and machinery equipment, electrical machinery and equipment, organic chemicals and chemical products, plastic, copper and articles thereof
Estonia	1,408,556	15.52 (2002 est)	11	4.99	Vegetables and fruits	Raw hides and skins, leather
Latvia	2,348,784	20.99 (2002 est)	8,9	11.68	Cereals	Fertilisers

Contd...

...Contd...

Country	*Population*	*GDP (PPP basis) in billion dollars*	*GDP per capita (PPP basis)*	*India's total trade in million (2002-03) dollars*	*Major items of from India*	*Major items of imports exports into India*
Lithuania	3,592,561	30.08(2002 est)	8,4	15.68	Cotton, pharmaceutical products, marine products	Fertilisers, copper and articles thereof
Hungary	10,045,407	134 (2002)	13,3	68.88	Apparel and clothing, organic chemicals, cotton	Electrical machinery and equipment, nuclear reactors, organic chemicals, paper and paper products
Slovak Republic	5,430,033	67.34	12,4	22.38	Footwear, articles of apparel and clothing	Nuclear reactors, boilers, organic chemicals
Malta	400,42	6.82	17,2	32.5	Minerals, cotton	Electrical machinery

Source: FICCI

References

Baldwin, Richard E., *Towards an Integrated Europe*, CEPR (Center for Economic Policy Resarch), London, 1994.

Boillot, Jean-Joseph and alii, "New Trade Geography of Eastern Europe," *Economic and Political Weekly* Vol. XXXIX No. 20, May 15-21, 2004, pp. 2001-2004 .Online www.epw.org.in

Boillot, Jean-Joseph and Nicolas Michelon, "The South China Triangle and Taiwan, From a Maquilladoras Zone to an Integrated Economy," *China Perspectives No.30*, July - August 2000, p. 32-37. Online www.cefc.com.hk/

Boillot, Jean-Joseph, "The New Economic Geography of Asia," *China Perspectives No. 30*, July - August 2000, pp. 18-25, www.cefc.com.hk/

Claudia M. Buch, Daniel Piazolo, "Capital and Trade Flows in Europe and the Impact of Enlargement," Kiel Institute of World Economics, *Kiel Working Paper, No. 1001*, September 2000.

Claudia M. Buch, Robert M. Kokta, Daniel Piazolo, 'Does the East Get What Would Otherwise Flow to the South? FDI Diversion in Europe', Kiel Institute of World Economics, *Kiel Working Paper, No. 1061*, July 2001.

Deutsches Institut für Wirtschaftsforschung (German institute for economic research), Wochenbericht 21/2000, May 25, 2000).

Economic Survey of Europe 2001, United Nations Economic Commission for Europe (UNECE), Geneva.

Edward Ky Chen, Chi Hung Kwan (eds), *Asia's Borderless Economy : The Emergence of Subregional Economic Zones*, Paul & Co. Publishers, Hong Kong, 1998

Ernst & Young, *European Investment Monitor, 2002* (and regular edition on their website)

European Barometer: Regular Pools Conducted for the European Commission, http://europa.eu.int/comm/public_opinion

European Commission, DG ECFIN, *The Economic Impact of Enlargement*, 2001.

European Commission, *Report on Cohesion*, Brussels 2001

European Commission, *Second Report on the Cohesion*, Brussels 2003

European Commission, *The Enlargement of the European Union, An historical opportunity*, accessible on the website : http://Europa.eu.int/comm/enlargement/

Eurostat, Statistics in brief, and a rich collection of statistics on http://europa.eu.int/comm/eurostat/

Fritiz Breuss, "Macroeconomic Effects of EU Enlargement for Old and New Members," *Wifo Working Paper*, 143/2001.

Jacques Rupnik, L'autre Europe, Le Seuil, Paris, 1993

Jakab, Zoltán M., Mihály A. Kovács, András Oszlay, "How Far Has Trade Integration Advanced ? An Analysis of the Actual and Potential Trade of Three Central and Eastern European Countries," *Journal of Comparative Economics*, Vol. 29, June 2001, pp. 276-292.

Krugman, Paul, *Geography and Trade*, Presses de l'Université de Louvain, Louvain 1991

Kornai, János, *The Road to a Free Economy. Shifting from a Socialist System: The Example of Hungary*. New York: W. W. Norton and Budapest, 1990

Lucas, Robert E., "Why Doesn't Capital Flow from Rich to Poor Countries ?," *American Economic Review*, Vol. 80, No. 2, May 1990, pp. 92-96.

Lamy, Pascal and Jean Pisani-Ferry, *L'Europe de nos volontés*, Plon, Paris, 2002.

Osterreichisches Institut für Wirtschaftsforschung, *Enlargement Paper, No. 4*, Munich 1998

Stiglitz, Joseph, *Globalization and its Discontents*, W. W. Norton & Company, New York, 2002.

UNCTAD, *World Investment Report*, UNCTAD, Geneva (yearly report)

World Economic Forum, *The Competitiveness Annual Report*, available on www.weforum.org

Xavier Richet, Frédéric Bourassa, "The Re-emergence of the Automotive Industry in Eastern Europe," in Christian von Hirschhausen, Jürgen Bitzer (eds.), *The Globalization of Industry and Innovation in Eastern Europe. From Post-Socialist Restructuring to International Competitiveness*, Edward Elgar Publishing, Cheltenham (United Kingdom), Northampton (United States), 2000, pp. 59-94.

Index

A

Accession Countries 156
Acquis communautaire 22, 24, 31, 65
Administrative capacity 31
Agricultural products 24, 153
Agriculture 28, 160
Albania 105
Alcatel 138
Alsace 106
Anti-dumping 160
Asia 89, 120
Attraction 60
Austria 61, 102, 114
Automobile 78, 79, 106, 145, 167
Automotive components 158
Aviation 167

B

Baltic sea belt 62
Baltic states 41, 88, 102, 141, 156
Banks 72
Barro, Robert 38
Belgium 153
Belt effect 100
Biotechnology 164
BMW 149
Brands 161
Brazil 70
Bucharest 76
Budapest 77
Budget 21, 48
Bulgaria 41, 54, 58, 104, 127
Burgundy 109
Business climate 159

C

Call centers 114
Capital goods 97
Carrefour 76
CEFTA 93, 95, 103
Central European belt 62
Chemicals 112, 153, 163
China 53, 101, 120, 139
Clothing see Textlie, see Textile
Cohesion 44
Comecon 95, 137
Common Agricultural Policy (CAP) 48
Compaq 138
Competition 128, 150, 164
Competitiveness 63
Components 146
Computer 137, 142
Consumer behaviour 75
Consumption 72
Consumption patterns 81
Convergence 37, 69, 117
Copenhagen criteria 16
Cosmetics 80
Croatia 76, 125
Cyprus 41, 55
Czech Republic 41, 54, 68, 76, 125, 129, 137, 144, 146, 153, 158

D

Dacia 115
Danone 95
Defense 158, 167
Dell 139
Delocalisation 22
Denmark 102
Domestic firms 68

E

EBRD 33
E-business 162
Economic geography 64
Economies of scale 46
Education 58
Electronics 111
Energy 96, 158
Enlargement 15
Entertainment 164
Estonia 54, 58, 141
EU Regulations 156
EU standards 159
European Commission 72
Exchange rates 75

F

FDI (Foreign Direct Investment) 35, 52, 158
Fiat 97, 149
FICCI 166
Finland 58, 102
Flextronics 68, 136
Food processing 159
Food products 78, 160
Foreign firms 68
France 72, 106, 108, 124, 132, 139, 150
Frankfurt 99
Free movement of persons 34
Fruits and vegetables 160
Furniture 78, 130, 158

G

Gems & jewellery 164
General Electric 138
Generic products 163
Geographical proximity 134
Germany 61, 72, 102, 114, 123, 153
Globalisation 45
Greece 38, 91, 104
Greenfield investments 69
GSP (Generalized System of Preferences) 162
GSP tariffs 158

H

Hungary 41, 54, 58, 76, 90, 103, 125, 130, 137, 144

I

Iberian peninsula 112
IBM 68, 137
Ikea 134
Ile-de-France 106
India 120, 139, 153, 158, 160
Institutional environment 59
Integration 86, 146, 101
Intellectual property rights 156
Intra-CEEC Trade 93
Ireland 38, 59, 90, 140
Iron and Steel 143
IT (or IT Information Technologies) 159
IT(NICT) 161
IT Services 163
Italy 72, 104, 114, 123, 146

J

Japan 60, 122

K

Kaname Akamatsu 104
Kornaï, Jànos 33
Krugman, Paul 55, 99, 115

Kyoto protocol 45

L

Labeling 160
Labour
semi-skilled 63
skilled 40, 128, 138
un-skilled 158
Labour costs 158, 163
Latin America 107
Latvia 54, 58
Leather product 153, 158
Leipzig 149
Leisure (expenditures) 80
Linkages 130, 153, 164
Lithuania 54, 58
Localisation 117, 150
Llocation 109, 158
London 99
Lorraine 108

M

Machine tools 158
Malta 41, 54
Mare Balticum 102
Marine Products 160
Mediterranean countries 122
Mediterranean zone 67
Metallurgy 158
Mexico 60, 64
Microsoft 136
Migration 36, 138
Mitteleuropa 102
Mobile (phone) 79, 140
Moscow 100
Motorola 137

N

Netherlands 62, 105
New Economic Geography 55, 99
Nice 19
NICT (or IT, Information Technologies) 109, 136
Nissan 107
Nokia 102, 138
Non-Tariff Barriers 165
Nordic countries 85, 114

O

OEM (Original Equipment Manufacturing) 136
OPT (Outward Processing Traffic) 129
Over-capacity 144

P

Paris 99
Patents 163
Pharmaceuticals 98, 163
Philips 138, 140
Poland 41, 54, 68, 76, 88, 102, 125, 130, 137, 143, 146, 153, 158
Polish belt 62
Porter, Michael 63
Portugal 29, 54, 91, 107, 123
Privatisation 79
Productivity 69, 71, 118
Productivity gap 69
Proximity 60, 137
PSA (Peugeot Automobile) 65, 109, 146, 151

Q

Qualification 138

R

R&D (Research and Development 63, 106, 119, 138, 141
Regional belts 99
Regional policy 28
Renault 52, 72, 115, 147
Restructuring 67
Retail sector 72
Revealed Comparative Advantages (RCA) 109
Romania 41, 54, 76, 104, 123, 127, 130, 138, 142, 149

Russia 85, 95

S

Sachs, Jeffrey 63
Samsung 137
Scandinavian countries 100
Schengen 166
Seat 108
Siemens 138
Silicon Valley 99
Skoda 52, 107
Slovakia 41, 54, 58, 144, 146
Slovenia 41, 54, 58, 76, 103, 104, 115, 141, 146
Sony 136
Southern European belt 103
Spain 29, 54, 89, 107, 123, 150
Specialisation 71, 109
Steel 111, 143, 167
Sub-contracting 133
Sweden 102, 139

T

Tariff advantage 158
Tariffs 156
Technological assimilation 63
Telecommunication operators 141
Textile 119, 125, 113, 153, 162
Tisco 77
Tobacco industry 68
Tourism 106, 164
Toyota 146
Trade 24
Trade barriers 165
Trade Creation Effect 155
Trade Diversion Effect 156
Trade documentation 154
Trade liberalization 156
Trade Regulations 156
Transition 85, 104, 117
Transition periods 19, 156
Transnational firms 115
Turkey 16, 53, 100, 105, 123, 150

U

UK 153, 161
Unemployment rate 69
United States 45, 60, 89, 115, 122, 139
Urban infrastructure 164

V

Videoton 68, 137
Visa 166
Volkswagen 72, 108, 147

W

Wages 56, 126
Warsaw 76, 127
Whisky 160
Women (professional activity) 82